New Directions for
Child and Adolescent
Development

Reed W. Larson
Lene Arnett Jensen
EDITORS-IN-CHIEF

William Damon
FOUNDING EDITOR

Core Competencies to Prevent Problem Behaviors and Promote Positive Youth Development

Nancy G. Guerra
Catherine P. Bradshaw
EDITORS

Number 122 • Winter 2008
Jossey-Bass
San Francisco

CORE COMPETENCIES TO PREVENT PROBLEM BEHAVIORS AND PROMOTE POSITIVE YOUTH DEVELOPMENT
Nancy G. Guerra, Catherine P. Bradshaw (eds.)
New Directions for Child and Adolescent Development, no. 122
Reed W. Larson, Lene Arnett Jensen, Editors-in-Chief

© 2008 Wiley Periodicals, Inc., A Wiley Company. All rights reserved.

No part of this publication may be reproduced, stored in a retrieval system, or transmitted in any form or by any means, electronic, mechanical, photocopying, recording, scanning, or otherwise, except as permitted under Sections 107 or 108 of the 1976 United States Copyright Act, without either the prior written permission of the Publisher or authorization through payment of the appropriate per-copy fee to the Copyright Clearance Center, 222 Rosewood Drive, Danvers, MA 01923; (978) 750-8400, fax (978) 646-8600. Requests to the Publisher for permission should be addressed to the Permissions Department, John Wiley & Sons, Inc., 111 River St., Hoboken, NJ 07030, (201) 748-6011, fax (201) 748-6008, www.wiley.com/go/permissions.

Microfilm copies of issues and articles are available in 16mm and 35mm, as well as microfiche in 105mm, through University Microfilms, Inc., 300 North Zeeb Road, Ann Arbor, Michigan 48106-1346.

ISSN 1520-3247   electronic ISSN 1534-8687

NEW DIRECTIONS FOR CHILD AND ADOLESCENT DEVELOPMENT is part of The Jossey-Bass Education Series and is published quarterly by Wiley Subscription Services, Inc., a Wiley company, at Jossey-Bass, 989 Market Street, San Francisco, California 94103-1741. Periodicals postage paid at San Francisco, California, and at additional mailing offices. Postmaster: Send address changes to New Directions for Child and Adolescent Development, Jossey-Bass, 989 Market Street, San Francisco, CA 94103-1741.

New Directions for Child and Adolescent Development is indexed in Cambridge Scientific Abstracts (CSA/CIG), CHID: Combined Health Information Database (NIH), Contents Pages in Education (T&F), Current Abstracts (EBSCO), Educational Research Abstracts Online (T&F), ERIC Database (Education Resources Information Center), Index Medicus/MEDLINE/PubMed (NLM), Linguistics & Language Behavior Abstracts (CSA/CIG), Psychological Abstracts/PsycINFO (APA), Social Services Abstracts (CSA/CIG), SocINDEX (EBSCO), and Sociological Abstracts (CSA/CIG).

SUBSCRIPTION rates: For the U.S., $85 for individuals and $280 for institutions. Please see ordering information page at end of journal.

EDITORIAL CORRESPONDENCE should be e-mailed to the editors-in-chief: Reed W. Larson (larsonr@uiuc.edu) and Lene Arnett Jensen (ljensen@clarku.edu).

Jossey-Bass Web address: www.josseybass.com

Contents

1. Linking the Prevention of Problem Behaviors and Positive Youth Development: Core Competencies for Positive Youth Development and Risk Prevention 1
Nancy G. Guerra, Catherine P. Bradshaw
This introductory chapter describes a set of core competencies (a positive sense of self, self-control, decision-making skills, a moral system of belief, and prosocial connectedness) that are important for promoting positive youth development and reducing at-risk behavior in youth.

2. Core Competencies and the Prevention of School Failure and Early School Leaving 19
Catherine P. Bradshaw, Lindsey M. O'Brennan, Clea A. McNeely
The authors highlight the importance of prosocial connectedness to the school environment, other youth, and parents in promoting success at school.

3. Core Competencies and the Prevention of Youth Violence 33
Terri N. Sullivan, Albert D. Farrell, Amie F. Bettencourt, Sarah W. Helms
The authors use a social-cognitive perspective to frame the role of the core competencies in the prevention of aggressive and violent behavior.

4. Core Competencies and the Prevention of Adolescent Substance Use 47
Tamara M. Haegerich, Patrick H. Tolan
This chapter adopts a developmental-ecological perspective and emphasizes the importance of a positive sense of self and self-control in reducing problem use of drugs and alcohol.

5. Core Competencies and the Prevention of High-Risk Sexual Behavior 61
Vignetta Eugenia Charles, Robert Wm. Blum
Research is summarized to illustrate the importance of effective decision making, a positive sense of self, and prosocial connectedness for the promotion of healthy romantic relationships in adolescence.

6. Programs and Policies That Promote Positive Youth Development and Prevent Risky Behaviors: An International Perspective 75
Sophie Naudeau, Wendy Cunningham, Mattias K. A. Lundberg, Linda McGinnis
The authors identify challenges that youth face in developing countries and recommend a set of policies and programs that are effective within these contexts.

7. Future Directions for Research on Core Competencies 89
Catherine P. Bradshaw, Nancy G. Guerra
This concluding commentary discusses the strengths and weaknesses of the core competency approach and suggests directions for future research and prevention programming.

INDEX 93

Guerra, N. G., & Bradshaw, C. P. (2008). Linking the prevention of problem behaviors and positive youth development: Core competencies for positive youth development and risk prevention. In N. G. Guerra & C. P. Bradshaw (Eds.), *Core competencies to prevent problem behaviors and promote positive youth development*. New Directions for Child and Adolescent Development, 122, 1–17.

1

Linking the Prevention of Problem Behaviors and Positive Youth Development: Core Competencies for Positive Youth Development and Risk Prevention

Nancy G. Guerra, Catherine P. Bradshaw

Abstract

In this chapter, we present a brief review of the developmental literature linking healthy adjustment to five core competencies: (1) positive sense of self, (2) self-control, (3) decision-making skills, (4) a moral system of belief, and (5) prosocial connectedness. A central premise of this chapter and the rest of the volume is that promoting mastery of social and emotional core competencies provides a connection between positive youth development and risk prevention programming. In subsequent chapters, empirical evidence linking these core competencies with prevention of specific risk behaviors is reviewed, and examples of integrated promotion and prevention efforts in the United States and internationally are discussed. © Wiley Periodicals, Inc.

Support for this project comes from the Centers for Disease Control and Prevention (5U49CE000734–04, 1U49CE 000728–011, and K01CE001333–01).

Adolescence generally is considered a time of experimentation and increased involvement in what have been called *risk behaviors* or *problem behaviors*, including school failure and early school leaving, youth violence, substance use, and high-risk sexual behavior (Biglan, Brennan, Foster, & Holder, 2004). Although most youth navigate this developmental stage relatively unscathed, risk behaviors for some youth become chronic, increasing the likelihood of adversity in multiple domains: physical health, life expectancy, psychosocial adjustment, and successful transition to adulthood (Jessor, 1992; Lindberg, Boggess, & Williams, 2000). School failure and early school leaving can lead to underemployment, violence can lead to criminal behavior, substance use can lead to addiction and related health problems, and risky sexual behavior can lead to sexually transmitted diseases and unplanned pregnancies.

Youth who are most likely to become regularly involved in one or more of these risk behaviors have been labeled *at-risk youth* or *youth at risk*. This increased chance of involvement can stem from individual characteristics of youth, the contexts they live in, the situations they encounter, and how these factors interact over time. A focus on at-risk youth has led to a proliferation of research highlighting the importance of discrete risk factors that increase the probability of risk behavior. In addition, research and practice have emphasized the role of protective factors that function to mitigate risk and can be considered promotive factors when they portend adjustment absent risk (Stouthamer-Loeber, Loeber, Wei, Farrington, & Wikström, 2002). Successful adaptation in the face of extreme stress has been labeled *resilience* (Masten & Coatsworth, 1998).

Drawing on research that has identified specific predictors and trajectories of risk, a multitude of small- and large-scale preventive interventions for specific risk behaviors have been developed, implemented, and evaluated (Biglan et al., 2004). Building on these efforts, practitioners and policymakers also have stressed the urgent need for coherent strategies and evidence-based programs that can be incorporated into large-scale federal initiatives in the United States (Ripple & Zigler, 2003). Concerns about youth at risk are international in scope (World Bank, 2006).

Carefully articulated and empirically supported models of youth risk behaviors have contributed significantly to the field of child and adolescent development over the past several decades. However, as these models began to shape community programs and policies for youth, conceptual and practical challenges emerged. From a pragmatic perspective, one of the principal challenges of a risk-focused approach is that it resulted in the proliferation of separate problem-specific programs, funded by independent agencies supporting work in each risk area, and disseminated through different publication venues (for example, substance abuse prevention programs funded by the National Institute on Drug Abuse with findings published in drug and alcohol specialty journals). Rather than emphasizing the identification of shared risk, protective, and promotive factors, both research and practice generally have treated adolescent risk behaviors as separate and independent, with little consideration of their interconnectedness and common causal pathways. This is somewhat surprising given high levels of covariation across risk behaviors in the United States (Barone et al., 1995) and internationally (Fergusson, Horwood, & Lynskey, 1994), and empirically supported theoretical models such as problem behavior theory that provide a coherent framework for understanding the common predictors of multiple risk or problem behaviors (Jessor & Jessor, 1977; Jessor et al., 2003).

A second challenge relates more generally to the vision of youth that emerged from a risk-focused approach. In recent years, a programmatic emphasis on youth at risk has been criticized for emphasizing what goes wrong rather than what goes right; this perspective portrays youth as problems to be fixed and development as a process of overcoming deficits and risk. As proponents of strength-based models have noted, a risk-focused approach can obscure the fact that adolescence also is a time of mastery linked to each child's unique talents, strengths, skills, and interests (Damon, 2004; Larson, 2000; Scales & Leffert, 2004). An emphasis on the positive and adaptive features of adolescence has been incorporated into a number of models generally subsumed under the rubric of *positive youth development*. From this perspective, successful development is viewed not as the absence of risk behavior but as the presence of positive attributes that enable youth to reach their full potential as productive and engaged adults (Lerner & Benson, 2003; Pittman & Irby, 1996).

Positive youth development models typically encompass a broad set of personal and contextual attributes for all youth, without identifying youth most in need or specifying whether and how specific youth strengths can mitigate risk. A number of these models have been articulated, each with specific implications for practice. One of the most widely used approaches is the developmental assets model promoted by the Search Institute (Benson, 1997). This model is built around forty developmental assets that reflect internal qualities such as positive values and external assets such as caring families and high community expectations for youth behavior (Scales & Leffert, 2004). A more focused effort within the developmental literature highlights the Five Cs youth need to thrive: cognitive and behavioral competence, confidence, positive social connections, character, and caring, leading to a sixth C of contribution to society (Lerner & Benson, 2003). Still other models focus primarily on engagement as a key marker of positive youth development, emphasizing the need to foster initiative (Larson, 2000) and involve youth as active contributors to their communities (Hughes & Curnan, 2000).

To some degree, risk prevention and positive youth development approaches have been portrayed as opposite and somewhat incompatible ends of a continuum (Small & Memmo, 2004). From a translational perspective, not only have risk-focused models emphasizing discrete behaviors led to separate interventions for separate problems, but a more general debate between problem-centered versus asset-building strategies often has forced schools and communities to choose between these two perspectives. Yet an either-or approach does little to address the reality of daily life: communities that want to embrace the talents and strengths of all youth also must address the very real problems of some youth that interfere with their own development as well as the lives of others. At this juncture, rather than pitting these approaches against each other, it is more useful (and cost-effective) for the field to emphasize their commonalities and specify how they can be integrated in order to meet the needs of all youth, including those at greatest risk. Building assets should not blind us to the importance of reducing adversity for youth most likely to experience negative outcomes. Even the most ardent proponents of youth development and asset building acknowledge the need to accentuate the positive in order to simultaneously minimize the negative (Hawkins, Catalano, Kosterman, Abbott, & Hill, 1999; Lerner & Benson, 2003).

Linking the promotion of positive development with the prevention of risk is conceptually appealing. As Masten and Coatsworth (1998, p. 216) comment, "Prevention at its best represents both an effort to foster competence and to prevent problems." Despite repeated calls over the years for integrated approaches (Cowen, 1973; Hawkins & Weis, 1985), efforts to develop comprehensive models to guide research and practice have been the exception. Still, considerable gains have been made in fostering a structured dialogue between prevention and promotion. For example, in the mid-1990s, the U.S. Department of Health and Human Services commissioned a large-scale report focused on positive youth development and its links to prevention of youth problem behaviors, *Positive Youth Development in the United States* (Catalano, Berglund, Ryan, Lonczak, & Hawkins, 1999). The report noted that twenty-four well-evaluated youth development programs resulted in significant reductions in a range of problem behaviors. However, definitions of positive youth development were linked to fifteen attributes of programs (such as promoting bonding or providing recognition for positive behavior) rather than characteristics of well-adjusted youth. Notably, the report did not specify the precise markers of adjustment for youth and how these attributes are linked specifically to risk behaviors.

This volume continues the dialogue by presenting a set of chapters written by accomplished developmental and prevention researchers with expertise in one or more youth risk behaviors. The overarching goal is to articulate a set of core social and emotional competencies that capture what it means to be a healthy youth (in other words, individual attributes that define positive outcomes) and to examine how these competencies are linked to specific risk behaviors and related preventive interventions and positive youth development programs in the United States and internationally.

Individual markers of adjustment are emphasized as outcomes, with careful consideration of how these competencies unfold over time as a result of the complex interactions across multiple levels of the social ecological system (Bronfenbrenner & Morris, 1998). Advances in prevention science and practice have underscored the need to consider how skills and competencies develop across multiple and intersecting developmental contexts, including families, peers, and communities (Eccles & Gootman, 2002; Guerra & Leidy, 2008).

Furthermore, these skills and competencies may have distinctive meanings within specific ethnic and cultural groups (Guerra & Smith, 2005). Consider a skill such as decision making. Although certain elements of decision-making skills, such as attention to relevant cues and generation of multiple alternative solutions, may be important cognitive-developmental milestones that are relevant across cultures, culturally appropriate decision making ultimately requires integration with relevant group values and practices. For example, in collectivistic societies such as Japan, interpersonal harmony and the avoidance of conflict are primary values against which the adaptive value of any decision will be judged (Markus & Kitayama, 1998). Similarly, within Latino culture, the value of *colectivismo* emphasizes the importance of subordinating personal desires to the interests of the group (Mirabel-Colon & Velez, 2005).

Skill-building interventions that go beyond direct instruction and address ecological influences that are important for development are more likely to have a preventive effect and promote positive adjustment (Metropolitan Area Child Study, 2002). Still, a central premise of this volume is that it is critical to articulate the precise individual competencies that are the ultimate targets of preventive interventions across the ecological spectrum and to examine the connections between promotion and prevention efforts.

Five Core Competencies

How do we know what set of core competencies best characterize a psychologically well-adjusted youth and can provide a foundation for preventive interventions to reduce risk behaviors? First, it is important to clarify the meaning of *competence* in relation to adolescent social and emotional adjustment. Construed broadly, competence reflects effective adaptation in a given environment. From a developmental standpoint, competence can be understood as mastery of key developmental tasks that signal effective adaptation within a particular life stage and as determined by a specific historical and cultural context (Havighurst, 1972). Over the years, multiple lists of major developmental tasks have been proposed (for a brief review, see Masten & Coatsworth, 1998). Across most lists, these tasks reflect broad domains of competence linked to specific age-appropriate behaviors (such as the ability to follow rules and get along with others when children enter school), as well as a range of skills and accomplishments. To date, there has not been a universally agreed-on list of key markers of adolescent development and adjustment, although certain competencies have received considerable attention in developmental and prevention research.

Based on a careful review of the literature and consensus among the authors of the chapters in this volume and a group of invited discussants at an all-day workshop, five core competencies were selected to provide a guiding framework for the chapters in this volume: (1) a positive sense of self, (2) self-control, (3) decision-making skills, (4) a moral system of belief, and (5) prosocial connectedness. Although these competencies clearly are interconnected (for instance, higher levels of self-control lead to better decision making), each has received substantial attention in its own right. They also are closely aligned with proposed assets and strengths from many of the youth development frameworks discussed previously. In addition, although there are other candidates for potential inclusion, these competencies capture important elements of evidence-based competence enhancement and prevention programs, for example, life skills training (Botvin, Mihalic, & Grotpeter, 1998) and aggression replacement training (Goldstein, 2004).

A central premise of this volume is that high levels of these competencies provide a marker for positive youth development, and low levels of these competencies increase the likelihood of adolescent risk behavior. To provide a background and context for connecting competencies with risk behavior and prevention, it is useful to define each competency and identify more specific empirical indicators, which are supported by the literature on healthy development and risk prevention. It is important to keep in mind that each of these competencies can be divided into subdimensions. Indeed, as we shall see in subsequent chapters, empirical studies linking risk behavior and a particular competency may be limited to a particular subdimension. We lay out the multiple and most salient components of each competency in relation to its potential for helping us understand adjustment and risk but acknowledge that coverage of each specific subdimension may be uneven.

A Positive Sense of Self. The self has long been an object of discourse and inquiry in the social sciences. Currently there is considerable agreement regarding the importance of the self in behavior and adjustment, although less clarity regarding which components of the self are most important, how the self is shaped through social interaction, and the functions that the self performs (for a contemporary and historical review of research on the self, see Harter, 2006). There are also many possible interpretations of what it means to have a "positive sense of self" in relation to adaptation and adjustment in adolescence. For the goals of this volume, we highlight three components of self that emerge early in development and exert considerable influence during adolescence and the transition to adulthood: self-awareness, agency, and self-esteem.

Self-awareness becomes evident by the second year of life, although some of the earliest forms of self-awareness have been noted soon after birth (Gibson, 1995). With developmental progress comes an increasingly differentiated and more complex self. Young children typically rely on concrete, observable features to describe themselves, incorporating psychological attributes as they get older. With the emergence of language, children begin to construct more enduring portraits of the self, developing a personal narrative or autobiographical memory that provides consistency to experiences of the self (Moore & Lemmon, 2001).

During adolescence, self-descriptions vary across different roles with different demands (for example, the demands of peers versus the demands of parents), leading to conflicting self-stories and a search for a coherent identity. Indeed, the resolution of this identity search, or "crisis," has long been considered a normative feature and primary developmental task of adolescence (Erikson, 1968). Self-awareness for youth encompasses not only an accurate assessment of their physical, psychological, and behavioral attributes but a more refined and integrated conceptualization of the self that lays the groundwork for one's future life course. "Who I am" sets the stage for the "Who I could become"—providing hopefulness, direction, and a sense of purpose. The construction of future possible selves as personalized representations of important life goals (what individuals could become, would like to become, or are afraid of becoming) gives further meaning to experience and motivates action (Cross & Markus, 1991). A positive sense of self during adolescence hinges on success in constructing and maintaining positive and realistic possible selves to motivate current and future behavior (just as negative possible selves can portend maladjustment).

Agency, a sense of volition over self-generated acts, provides the motor for action. As early as infancy, individuals derive great pleasure from the recognition that they can control certain environmental events, such as throwing a ball on the floor or moving parts of a toy, and they respond negatively when these contingencies are interrupted (Watson, 1985). An important component of self-development is the increasing realization over time that the self is an active, independent agent, just as others are active, independent agents in their own lives. This forms the basis for a sense of self-efficacy, defined as people's beliefs about their capabilities to produce designated levels of performance that exercise influence over relevant events in their lives. A positive and strong sense of self-efficacy enhances adjustment and well-being as individuals set challenging goals, sustain efforts, and recover in the face of failure (Bandura, 1994). Absent self-efficacy for positive events (such as belief in one's ability to get good grades in school), individuals may build self-confidence by developing beliefs in their capabilities for negative events (such as the ability to bully others and act aggressively).

Self-esteem is both a widely cited and controversial marker of positive adjustment (Baumeister, Campbell, Krueger, & Vohs, 2003). At first blush, it is difficult even to define self-esteem. It has been used to refer to global judgments of self-worth that emerge around middle childhood, as well as domain-specific evaluations of different aspects of the self that become increasingly differentiated from childhood through adolescence and adulthood (Harter, 1990). Both global and domain-specific self-esteem may also be considered traits that are relatively stable over time or states that fluctuate in response to immediate conditions. In recent years, there has been a shift to hierarchical models that incorporate both global and domain-specific self-esteem. Individuals judge themselves across multiple domains, with global self-esteem reflecting a general self-evaluation that provides a type of composite assessment across these domains.

People also differ in the relative salience of domain-specific evaluations for their overall or global self-esteem (Crocker & Wolfe, 2001). For instance, some adolescents may consider academic performance important to their self-worth. In contrast, other teenagers may disengage self-esteem from their performance at school, focusing more on athletic abilities, popularity with peers, or more problematic talents such as power and superiority over others. Individuals also are more likely to gravitate to settings that provide opportunities to enhance self-esteem in relevant domains. Academically oriented students are likely to seek out educational opportunities, whereas youth whose self-esteem is contingent on power and aggression are more likely to seek out juvenile gangs.

High self-esteem is an important developmental goal associated with multiple indexes of positive affect and life satisfaction (Diener, 1984). However, understanding the links with positive and negative behaviors may require a more detailed understanding of how self-esteem is defined, what it is based on, and how it is realized. In other words, healthy adjustment should be related not only to the overall level of self-esteem but to the specific domains on which it is contingent and related opportunities for engagement and success in these domains. Just as socially valued contingencies contribute to positive development, the wrong contingencies (or lack of opportunities to satisfy even positive contingencies in socially acceptable ways) can contribute to one or more risk behaviors.

Self-Control. From an early age, children become increasingly adept at self-control, defined broadly as the ability to regulate and manage affect and behavior in a controlled versus automatic fashion in accordance with situational or normative demands. Self-control is evident when children follow rules they might rather disobey; inhibit their desire for immediate gratification, particularly in the presence of a tempting reward; and modulate responses in accordance with age-graded standards. A further distinction has been made between emotion regulation of internal feeling states and behavioral regulation of actions as two distinct components of self-control (Thompson, 1994).

Significant advances in self-control emerge during the preschool years in tandem with advances in general cognitive abilities, the control of attention, and emergent selfhood (Kopp, 1982). Early in development, children still control their behavior primarily in response to environmental contingencies such as punishment and reinforcement. They resist the temptation to take a coveted toy when an adult is present, but frequently grab the same toy as soon as the adult leaves the room. Over time, children internalize standards, which requires less external monitoring and more internal management (Bandura, 1991). However, brain maturation linked to self-control continues to develop through the adolescent years, as demonstrated in recent studies of brain activity showing that frontal lobe activation, an important determinant of behavioral inhibition, increases between adolescence and adulthood (Giedd et al., 1999; Steinberg, 2008). In addition to developmental progressions in self-control skills, there are individual temperamental, neurobiological, and caregiving contributions to the development of individual differences in self-control (Thompson, 2006).

Self-control is critical for individual adaptation as well as the structure and function of various sociocultural groups; organized groups and social institutions persist in part because of shared compliance to a set of standards. At the individual level, self-control is a prerequisite for goal-oriented behavior across multiple domains. An adolescent who wants to lose weight must exert self-control to inhibit a competing desire to eat chocolate cake. A student who wants to get a good grade on a test must inhibit a competing desire to stay out late with friends. Sustained relationships often require learning how to regulate negative emotions such as anger in a constructive fashion. Some evidence suggests that self-control may actually be a limited resource that can become depleted if used too often (Muraven & Baumeister, 2000).

From a developmental perspective, interest in self-control initially emerged from the study of dysregulation. In other words, why do some children resist parental requests or seem to be unable to wait their turn? Much of this work focused on the origins of self-regulation in young children and associated problems, with less attention focused on self-control during adolescence and its relation to adjustment. Most of the work on self-control during childhood and adolescence has emphasized the relation of low self-control to risk behaviors such as aggression (Caspi, Henry, McGee, Moffitt, & Silva, 1995) and criminality (Gottfredson & Hirschi, 1990) rather than its role in adaptation. More recently, Lerner and colleagues have examined the relation between self-control and both positive developmental outcomes and risk behaviors, providing empirical evidence that adolescent self-control, as measured by goal setting and goal pursuit, is positively related to indicators of both adjustment and risk (Gestsdottir & Lerner, 2007).

Decision-Making Skills. The transition from childhood to adolescence is characterized by increasing autonomy and opportunities for choices independent of adults. Many of the daily and long-term decisions youth make during adolescence affect their current and future well-being, including their social relationships, academic performance, and future opportunities. The capacity to make effective decisions also increases during this time with the development of more sophisticated abstract reasoning skills and a growing capacity for probabilistic reasoning. By adolescence, individuals are capable of imagining future outcomes in the present, coordinating independent pieces of information, and understanding the likelihood of various consequences occurring. Still, compared to adults, children and adolescents are less adept at several components of decision making: they are less able to plan for or anticipate the future, generate consequences spontaneously, learn from negative consequences, or view negative consequences as harmful (Reyna & Farley, 2006).

There have been several approaches to studying decision making during childhood and adolescence. Different decision-making frameworks have been used to study relations with different types of behavior. For instance, decision theory, emphasizing discrete steps such as listing choices, identifying consequences, and evaluating these consequences, has been used to study different types of adolescent risk behavior (Beyth-Marom, Austin, Fischhoff, Palmgren, & Jacobs-Quadrel, 1993). Studies have focused on characteristics of adolescent decision making linked to risk such as accuracy of risk perceptions and perceived vulnerability. In general, when compared with adults, adolescents overestimate risk and are just as likely to feel vulnerable. The most notable difference is that perceived benefits, as opposed to risks, are more likely to drive decisions. Furthermore, rather than carefully mulling over risks and benefits, better decision makers tend to rely on "gist-based" thinking in which they categorically avoid dangerous risks (Reyna & Farley, 2006).

A variation on decision theory emphasizes multiple components of mature decision making as related to responsible and irresponsible behaviors. Rather than focus on discrete decision-making processes, research on maturity of judgment emphasizes multiple components of effective decision making linked to individual qualities, including responsibility (self-reliance and autonomy), perspective (concern about consequences and impact on others), and temperance (self-control). In general, maturity of judgment has been found to increase with age and correlate with and predict more responsible decisions (Steinberg & Cauffman, 1996).

Social information processing is another decision-making framework based on sequential processing of information related to social situations. Although social information-processing models have been applied to risk behaviors such as aggression and violence, they are essentially models of social competence and have been used extensively in developmental research. They have been applied to ongoing decisions involved in social interactions, with studies examining how steps of social information processing affect adjustment. One of the most comprehensive and widely cited models was proposed by Dodge and colleagues (Crick & Dodge, 1994). This model builds on previous work examining goal setting, response generation, consequential thinking, and attributional biases and integrates other studies that have placed more emphasis on underlying rule structures and scripts children learn across multiple ecological settings (Guerra & Huesmann, 2004). To date, there is considerable empirical evidence suggesting that when faced with problematic social situations, well-adjusted children (those who are well behaved and well liked by peers) attend to an array of social cues and interpret those cues in an unbiased fashion, select appropriate goals, access and generate positive responses, consider consequences, and enact prosocial behaviors. Furthermore, this cognitive and behavioral pattern becomes increasingly automatic over time (Huesmann, 1998).

A Moral System of Belief. Morality is constructed by the child over time through social experiences shaped by cognitive-developmental abilities that increase with age. Although the very nature of morality has been debated for centuries (What is morality? What is the moral course of action?), an essential component involves internalized beliefs about how people in a society should behave in relation to others. Moral cognition encompasses judgments about moral issues such as harm, fairness, integrity, and responsibility, and it engages psychological process such as perspective taking and empathy (Guerra, Nucci, & Huesmann, 1994).

Developmental evidence suggests that the capacity for moral behavior is present during infancy. Infants show distress and pleasure in response to signals from caregivers and soon learn to comfort others in distress (Hoffman, 2000). These emotional dispositions are universal, although there is some variability in degree. Socialization experiences during childhood and adolescence affect how these capacities are codified into a particular moral belief system reflecting family, community, and cultural values. There is also variability in the salience of these moral belief systems for an adolescent's developing identity. Just as self-esteem is dependent on particular contingencies of self-worth (Crocker & Wolfe, 2001), individuals also differ on the centrality of moral beliefs to their developing sense of self, labeled their *moral identity*. As Damon (2004) and others have noted, moral identity may be the cement that binds moral thinking to moral action. In other words, if young people endorse a moral course of action and believe that it is essential to their identity, they ought to act accordingly (Nisan, 1996).

An emphasis on the development of a moral system of belief accompanied by a strong sense of moral identity has been a cornerstone of many positive youth development models. The forty developmental assets promoted by the Search Institute (Benson, 1997) include qualities with clear moral components: responsibility, restraint, caring, social justice, integrity, and honesty. Similarly, character education programs such as Character Counts emphasize personal qualities such as trustworthiness, respect, responsibility, fairness, caring, and citizenship. To the extent that specific risk behaviors involve potential harm to others (clearly violence, although one can argue that all risk behaviors have the potential for harm to those in the adolescent's immediate social circle as well as to society), moral identity is an important competency for positive youth development.

Prosocial Connectedness. The concept of connectedness has been used widely in the positive youth development literature, although there has been relatively little theoretical and empirical consistency in how it is defined. Terms such as *investment, engagement, attachment, bonding, sense of belonging,* and *mattering* all have been used to describe youth affiliations across a range of socialization domains, including families, schools, and communities. What these terms have in common is an overarching focus on a psychological state of belonging where individual youth perceive that they and others are cared for, acknowledged, trusted, and empowered within a given context (Eccles & Gootman, 2002; Whitlock, 2006). This state of belonging works both ways: connectedness involves both feeling cared for and caring about the social environment. These perceptions should be unmistakably linked to specific qualities of social contexts, but they are still individual perceptions consistent with the core competencies framework. Even the most welcoming contexts may alienate some youth if the fit between individual personal and developmental needs is askew (Eccles & Midgely, 1993).

The developmental literature suggests that individuals are genetically prewired to develop social attachments, beginning with the early bond between infants and their caregivers (Bowlby, 1969). These early attachments lead to internal working models of social relationships that serve as preliminary rules to guide both behavior and feelings in social interactions (for instance, that others can be trusted). The effects of positive and secure attachments appear to be far reaching and long lasting, with attachment quality predicting adjustment differences across multiple contexts and at later periods. Specifically, more secure patterns of early attachment predict higher levels of competence across domains and well into adolescence (Jacobsen, Edelstein, & Hofman, 1994).

Although a significant amount of developmental research has emphasized early connections with caregivers and among family members, as children grow up, they are progressively exposed to a range of social groups and contexts that influence adjustment. Their lives are intertwined with multiple peer groups, including friends, romantic partners, siblings, neighborhood children, cliques, classmates, and, most recently, a virtual online social world. They are involved with adults other than parents and relatives as they navigate different institutions and settings, including youth groups, religious organizations, and schools (Beam, Chen, & Greenberger, 2002). Each of these social ecologies carries with it multiple opportunities for participation and connectedness, just as they can portend withdrawal and alienation.

As several recent reviews have noted, youth connectedness across these multiple domains is a primary determinant of adjustment (Commission on Children at Risk, 2003) and also predicts risk taking in certain areas, such as high-risk sexual behavior (Kirby, 2001). Because schools are a primary developmental context for most children in the United States and internationally, a growing body of research has emphasized the importance of school connectedness in positive youth development and how it changes across elementary, middle, and high school (McNeeley, Nonnemaker, & Blum, 2002). Although shifts in organizational structure of schools in the United States, particularly in middle school, have been designed in part to increase student belonging and connectedness, research suggests that perceptions of school connectedness actually decrease in a linear fashion, with high school students reporting the lowest levels (WestEd, 2001).

Connectedness requires both opportunities and skills. Affluent settings typically are characterized by an abundance of opportunities for engagement, whereas resource-poor communities often struggle to provide meaningful connections for youth. Nevertheless, many opportunities for social engagement require a certain level of skill and motivation. Students who do well academically are more likely to be engaged in school life, athletic abilities are needed for most sports teams, musical aptitude is required for sustained involvement in band and orchestra, engagement with peers requires social skills, and so on. Furthermore, although skilled youth are more likely to be engaged and connected to social groups and institutions, youth with fewer skills and opportunities nevertheless find ways to belong. Virtual video game communities, Internet chatrooms, deviant peer groups, and youth gangs all provide at least some opportunity for connectedness. Belonging in and of itself, although psychologically rewarding, is unlikely to be associated with positive youth development and low levels of risk behaviors unless youth belong to prosocial groups.

Overview of the Volume

Taken together, the research suggests that these five competencies play an important role in the promotion of positive youth development and prevention of risk. The remaining chapters in this volume link these core competencies with the prevention of four broad types of risk behavior. Catherine Bradshaw, Lindsey O'Brennan, and Clea McNeely in Chapter Two examine the five competencies in relation to the prevention of school failure and early school leaving. They emphasize the critical role of prosocial connectedness to the school environment, other youth, and parents in promoting success at school. In Chapter Three, Terri Sullivan, Albert Farrell, Amie Bettencourt, and Sarah Helms consider the relation between the competencies and the prevention of youth violence. Their review underscores the utility of the social-cognitive perspective in understanding the role of the core competencies in youth violence. Tamara Haegerich and Patrick Tolan apply the core competencies framework to the prevention of adolescent substance use in Chapter Four. By adopting a developmental-ecological perspective, their work illustrates the importance of positive sense of self and self-control in reducing use of drugs and alcohol. In Chapter Five, Vignetta Charles and Robert Blum explore the association among the core competencies and the prevention of high-risk sexual behavior. Their work highlights the importance of effective decision making, a positive sense of self, and prosocial connectedness for promoting healthy romantic relationships in adolescence.

Each chapter summarizes the empirical literature linking the five core competencies to the risk behavior, provides examples from developmental and prevention research, and identifies areas for future research on promotion of the core competencies. The authors highlight programs and policies that have changed one or more core competencies through efforts designed to build individual skills, strengthen relationships, and enhance opportunities and supports across multiple developmental contexts.

In Chapter Six, Sophie Naudeau, Wendy Cunningham, Mattias Lundberg, and Linda McGinnis provide a broader, international perspective on positive youth development and prevention of risk behaviors, with examples of comprehensive policies and programs around the world. They identify a set of practical recommendations for policymakers in promoting the core competencies. The volume concludes with a brief commentary on the core competencies framework and the chapters focused on the four risk behaviors. We discuss the strengths and limitations of this framework and identify areas for future research linking positive youth development and risk prevention.

References

Bandura, A. (1991). Self-regulation of motivation through anticipatory and self-regulatory mechanisms. In R. A. Dienstbier (Ed.), *Perspectives on motivation: Nebraska Symposium on Motivation* (Vol. 38, pp. 79–94). Lincoln: University of Nebraska Press.

Bandura, A. (1994). Self-efficacy. In V. S. Ramachaudran (Ed.), *Encyclopedia of human behavior* (Vol. 4, pp. 71–81). Orlando, FL: Academic Press.

Barone, C., Weissberg, R. P., Kasprow, W. J., Voyce, C. K., Arthur, M. W., & Shriver, T. P. (1995). Involvement in multiple problem behaviors of young urban adolescents. *Journal of Primary Prevention, 15*, 261–283.

Baumeister, R. F., Campbell, J. D., Krueger, J. I., & Vohs, K. D. (2003). Does high self-esteem cause better performance, interpersonal success, happiness, or healthier lifestyles? *Psychological Science in the Public Interest, 4*, 1–44.

Beam, M. R., Chen, C., & Greenberger, E. (2002). The nature of adolescents' relationships with their "very important" nonparental adults. *American Journal of Community Psychology, 30*, 305–325.

Benson, P. (1997). *All kids are our kids.* San Francisco: Jossey-Bass.

Beyth-Maron, R., Austin, L., Fischhoff, B., Palmgren, C., & Jacobs-Quadrel, M. (1993). Perceived consequences of risky behaviors: Adults and adolescents. *Developmental Psychology, 29*, 226–236.

Biglan, A., Brennan, P. A., Foster, S. L., & Holder, H. D. (Eds.). (2004). *Helping adolescents at risk: Prevention of multiple problem behaviors.* New York: Guilford Press.

Botvin, G. J., Mihalic, S. F., & Grotpeter, J. K. (1998). *Life skills training: Blueprints for violence prevention, Book Five.* Boulder: University of Colorado, Center for the Study and Prevention of Violence, Institute of Behavioral Science.

Bowlby, J. (1969). *Attachment and loss: Vol. 1. Attachment.* New York: Basic Books.

Bronfenbrenner, U., & Morris, P. (1998). The ecology of developmental processes. In W. Damon (Ed.), *Handbook of child psychology, Vol. 1. Theoretical models of human development* (pp. 993–1028). Hoboken, NJ: Wiley.

Caspi, A., Henry, G., McGee, R. O., Moffitt, T. E., & Silva, P. A. (1995). Temperamental origins of child and adolescent behavior problems. *Child Development, 66*, 55–68.

Catalano, R. F., Berglund, M. L., Ryan, J.A.M., Lonczak, H. S., & Hawkins, J. D. (1999). *Positive youth development in the United States.* Washington, DC: U.S. Department of Health and Human Services.

Commission on Children at Risk. (2003). *Hardwired to connect: The new scientific case for authoritative communities.* New York: Institute for American Values.
Cowen, E. L. (1973). Social and community interventions. *Annual Review of Psychology, 24,* 423–472.
Crick, N. R., & Dodge, K. A. (1994). A review and reformulation of social information-processing mechanisms in children's social adjustment. *Psychological Bulletin, 115,* 74–101.
Crocker, J., & Wolfe, C. T. (2001). Contingencies of self-worth. *Psychological Review, 108,* 595–623.
Cross, S., & Markus, H. (1991). Possible selves across the life span. *Human Development, 34,* 230–255.
Damon, W. (2004). What is positive youth development? *Annals of the American Academy of Political and Social Science, 591,* 13–24.
Diener, E. (1984). Subjective well-being. *Psychological Bulletin, 95,* 542–575.
Eccles, J., & Gootman, J. (Eds.). (2002). *Community programs to promote youth development.* Washington, DC: National Academy Press.
Eccles, J., & Midgely, C. (1993). Development during adolescence: The impact of stage-environment fit on young adolescent experience in school and in families. *American Psychologist, 48,* 90–101.
Erikson, E. (1968). *Identity, youth, and society.* New York: Norton.
Fergusson, D. M., Horwood, L. J., & Lynskey, M. T. (1994). The comorbidities of adolescent problem behaviors: A latent class model. *Journal of Abnormal Child Psychology, 22,* 339–354.
Gestsdottir, S., & Lerner, R. M. (2007). Intentional self-regulation and positive youth development in early adolescence: Findings from the 4-H study of positive youth development. *Developmental Psychology, 43,* 508–521.
Gibson, E. (1995). Are we automata? In P. Rochat (Ed.), *The self in infancy* (pp. 3–15). Amsterdam: North Holland-Elsevier.
Giedd, J. N., Blumenthal, J., Jeffries, N. O., Castellanos, F. X., Liu, H., Zijdenbos, A., et al. (1999). Brain development during childhood and adolescence: A longitudinal MRI study. *Nature, 2,* 861–863.
Goldstein, A. P. (2004). Evaluations of effectiveness. In A. P. Goldstein, R. Nensen, B. Daleflod, & M. Kalt (Eds.), *New perspectives on aggression replacement training* (pp. 230–244). Hoboken, NJ: Wiley.
Gottfredson, M. R., & Hirschi, T. (1990). *A general theory of crime.* Stanford, CA: Stanford University Press.
Guerra, N. G., & Huesmann, L. R. (2004). A cognitive-ecological model of aggression. *Revue Internationale de Psychologie Sociale, 17,* 177–203.
Guerra, N. G., & Leidy, M. (2008). Lessons learned: Recent advances in understanding and preventing childhood aggression. In R. Kail (Ed.), *Advances in child development and behavior* (pp. 287–330). Orlando, FL: Academic Press.
Guerra, N. G., Nucci, L., & Huesmann, L. R. (1994). Moral cognition and childhood aggression. In L. R Huesmann (Ed.), *Current perspectives in aggressive behavior* (pp. 13–33). New York: Plenum.
Guerra, N. G., & Smith, E. P. (Eds.). (2005). *Preventing youth violence in a multicultural society.* Washington, DC: APA Books.
Harter, S. (1990). Causes, correlates and the functional role of global self-worth: A life-span perspective. In J. Kolligian & R. Sternberg (Eds.), *Perceptions of competence and incompetence across the life span* (pp. 67–98). New Haven, CT: Yale University Press.
Harter, S. (2006). The self. In W. Damon (series ed.), *Handbook of child psychology, Vol. 3. Social, emotional, and personality development* (6th ed., pp. 505–570). Hoboken, NJ: Wiley.
Havighurst, R. J. (1972). *Developmental tasks and education* (3rd ed.). New York: McKay.

Hawkins, J. D., Catalano, R. F., Kosterman, R., Abbott, R., & Hill, K. G. (1999). Preventing adolescent health-risk behaviors by strengthening protection during childhood. *Archives of Pediatric Adolescent Medicine, 153,* 226–234.

Hawkins, J. D., & Weis, J. G. (1985). The social development model: An integrated approach to delinquency prevention. *Journal of Primary Prevention, 6,* 73–97.

Hoffman, M. (2000). *Empathy and moral development: Implications for caring and justice.* Cambridge: Cambridge University Press.

Huesmann, L. R. (1998). The role of social information processing and cognitive schema in the acquisition and maintenance of habitual aggressive behavior. In R. Geen & E. Donnerstein (Eds.), *Human aggression* (pp. 73–109). Orlando, FL: Academic Press.

Hughes, D., & Curnan, S. (2000). Community youth development: A framework for action. *Community Youth Development Journal, 1,* 9–13.

Jacobsen, T., Edelstein, W., & Hofman, V. (1994). A longitudinal study of the relation between representatives of attachment in childhood and cognitive functioning in childhood and adolescence. *Developmental Psychology, 30,* 112–124.

Jessor, R. (1992). Risk behavior in adolescence: A psychosocial framework for understanding and action. *Developmental Review, 12,* 374–390.

Jessor, R., & Jessor, S. L. (1977). *Problem behavior and psychosocial development: A longitudinal study of youth.* Orlando, FL: Academic Press.

Jessor, R., Turbin, M. S., Costa, F. M., Dong, Q., Zhang, H., & Wang, C. (2003). Adolescent problem behavior in China and the United States: A cross-national study of psychosocial protective factors. *Journal of Research on Adolescence, 13,* 329–360.

Kirby, D. (2001). Understanding what works and what doesn't in reducing adolescent risk-taking. *Family Planning Perspectives, 33,* 276–281.

Kopp, C. B. (1982). Antecedents of self regulation: A developmental perspective. *Developmental Psychology, 18,* 199–214.

Larson, R. W. (2000). Toward a psychology of positive youth development. *American Psychologist, 55,* 170–183.

Lerner, R. M., & Benson, P. I. (2003). *Developmental assets and asset-building communities: Implications for research, policy, and practice.* New York: Kluwer Academic/Plenum.

Lindberg, L. D., Boggess, S., & Williams, S. (2000). *Multiple threats: The co-occurrence of teen health risk behaviors.* Washington, DC: Urban Institute.

Markus, H., & Kitayama, S. (1998). The cultural psychology of personality. *Journal of Cross-Cultural Psychology, 29,* 32–61.

Masten, A. S., & Coatsworth, J. D. (1998). The development of competence in favorable and unfavorable environments: Lessons from research on successful children. *American Psychologist, 53,* 205–220.

McNeeley, C. A., Nonnemaker, J. M., & Blum, R. W. (2002). Promoting school connectedness: Evidence from the National Longitudinal Study of Adolescent Health. *Journal of School Health, 72,* 138–146.

Metropolitan Area Child Study. (2002). A cognitive-ecological approach to preventing aggression in urban settings: Initial outcomes for high-risk children. *Journal of Consulting and Clinical Psychology, 70,* 179–194.

Mirabel-Colon, B., & Velez, C. (2005). Youth violence prevention among Latino youth. In N. G. Guerra & E. Phillips-Smith (Eds.), *Preventing youth violence in a multicultural society* (pp. 103–126). Washington, DC: APA Books.

Moore, C., & Lemmon, K. (Eds.). (2001). *The self in time.* Mahway, NJ: Erlbaum.

Muraven, M., & Baumeister, R. F. (2000). Self-regulation and depletion of limited resources: Does self-control resemble a muscle? *Psychological Bulletin, 126,* 247–259.

Nisan, M. (1996). Personal identity and education for the desirable. *Journal of Moral Education, 25,* 75–84.

Pittman, K., & Irby, M. (1996). *Preventing problems or promoting development: Competing priorities or inseparable goals?* Baltimore, MD: International Youth Foundation.

Reyna, V. F., & Farley, F. (2006). Risk and rationality in adolescent decision making: Implications for theory, practice, and public policy. *Psychological Science in the Public Interest, 7,* 1–49.

Ripple, C. H., & Zigler, E. (2003). Research, policy, and the federal role in prevention initiatives for children. *American Psychologist, 58,* 482–490.

Scales, P. C., & Leffert, N. (2004). *Developmental assets: A synthesis of the scientific research on adolescent development* (2nd ed.). Minneapolis, MN: Search Institute.

Small, S., & Memmo, M. (2004). Contemporary models of youth development and problem prevention: Toward an integration of terms, concepts, and models. *Family Relations, 53,* 3–11.

Steinberg, L. (2008). A social neuroscience perspective on adolescent risk-taking. *Developmental Review, 28,* 78–106.

Steinberg, L., & Cauffman, E. (1996). Maturity of judgment in adolescence: Psychosocial factors in adolescent decision making. *Law and Human Behavior, 20,* 249–272.

Stouthamer-Loeber, M., Loeber, R., Wei, E., Farrington, D. P., & Wikström, P. H. (2002). Risk and promotive effects in the explanation of persistent serious delinquency in boys. *Journal of Consulting and Clinical Psychology, 70,* 111–123.

Thompson, R. A. (1994). Emotional regulation: A theme in search of definition. *Monographs of the Society for Research in Child Development, 59* (2–3, Serial No. 240), 25–52.

Thompson, R. A. (2006). The development of the person: Social understanding, relationships, self, conscience. In W. Damon (series ed.), *Handbook of child psychology, Vol. 3. Social, emotional, and personality development* (6th ed.). Hoboken, NJ: Wiley.

Watson, J. (1985). Contingency perception in early social development. In T. Field & N. Fox (Eds.), *Social perception in infants* (pp. 157–176). Norwood, NJ: Ablex.

WestEd. (2001). *California Healthy Kids Survey: Resilience module spring 2000 report.* Los Alamitos, CA: WestEd California Healthy Kids Program Office.

Whitlock, J. (2006). Youth perceptions of life at school: Contextual correlates of school connectedness in adolescence. *Applied Developmental Science, 10,* 13–29.

World Bank. (2006). *Development and the next generation.* Washington, DC: World Bank.

NANCY G. GUERRA *is a professor and the director of the Academic Center for Excellence in Youth Violence Prevention at the University of California, Riverside.*

CATHERINE P. BRADSHAW *is an assistant professor and the associate director for the Johns Hopkins Center for the Prevention of Youth Violence at the Johns Hopkins Bloomberg School of Public Health.*

Bradshaw, C. P., O'Brennan, L. M., & McNeely, C. A. (2008). Core competencies and the prevention of school failure and early school leaving. In N. G. Guerra & C. P. Bradshaw (Eds.), *Core competencies to prevent problem behaviors and promote positive youth development. New Directions for Child and Adolescent Development, 122,* 19–32.

2

Core Competencies and the Prevention of School Failure and Early School Leaving

Catherine P. Bradshaw, Lindsey M. O'Brennan, Clea A. McNeely

Abstract

There is an increasing awareness that school failure and early school leaving are processes, rather than discrete events, that often co-occur and can have lasting negative effects on children's development. Most of the literature has focused on risk factors for failure and dropout rather than on the promotion of competencies that can increase youths' likelihood of successfully completing high school. This chapter applies the core competencies framework to the promotion of youths' success within the school environment. We conclude with a brief review of evidence-based prevention strategies that address the five competencies and identify avenues for future research. © Wiley Periodicals, Inc.

Support for this project comes from the Centers for Disease Control and Prevention (1U49CE 000728–011 and K01CE001333–01). We thank Katrina Debnam and Greta Massetti for their comments on this chapter.

Although national data indicate that the percentage of American high school students who dropped out of high school declined from 15 percent in 1972 to a low of 9 percent in 2006 (Institute of Education Sciences, 2008), preventing early school leaving and academic failure continue to be two of the biggest challenges facing the American education system. Approximately 6 percent of White youth, 11 percent of Black youth, and 22 percent of Hispanic youth did not complete high school in 2006, and the rates were higher among foreign-born youth and youth in urban communities. Much of the apparent racial difference is likely due to socioeconomic differences among racial groups (Battin-Pearson et al., 2000). There are also gender differences, with boys showing elevated rates of dropout: 10 percent for boys versus 8 percent for girls (Institute of Education Sciences, 2008). Youth with educational disabilities and co-occurring social-emotional or mental health problems are also at increased risk for school failure and early school leaving (French & Conrad, 2001).

Academic problems are one of the most robust predictors of high school dropout (Newcomb et al., 2002); therefore, we cannot consider school dropout without simultaneously addressing academic problems. Although it is often difficult to tease apart causes from consequences, youth who are unsuccessful in school or drop out are at increased risk for displaying social-emotional problems (Prevatt & Kelly, 2003), engaging in delinquent and criminal behavior (Lochner & Moretti, 2004), displaying health-compromising behaviors such as drug use or risky sexual behavior (Garnier, Stein, & Jacobs, 1997), and having limited economic opportunities (Vernez, Krop, & Rydell, 1999). From a developmental perspective, children who leave school early may not be emotionally, socially, or cognitively mature enough to take on adult roles and responsibilities, such as working full time, establishing financial independence, and developing autonomy from the family (Arnett, 2000). Similarly, youth who drop out of school have a difficult time securing and maintaining stable employment and, on average, earn far less than high school graduates. The employment rate for high school graduates is approximately 71 percent, compared to about 50 percent of high school dropouts. On average, high school dropouts earn just 65 percent of the median U.S. earnings (Vernez et al., 1999).

This chapter applies the core competency framework (a positive sense of self, self-control, decision-making skills, a moral system of belief, and prosocial connectedness) proposed in Chapter One of this volume to the promotion of youths' success at school. We consider general theories relevant to the prevention of school failure and dropout, as well as the significance of the five core competencies at multiple ecological levels. We then shift our focus to evidence-based prevention and intervention strategies that address these core competencies as a method for promoting success at school and the completion of high school.

Theoretical Perspectives on Early School Leaving and School Failure

School failure and early school leaving are complex processes that often co-occur with each other and with several of the other problem behaviors examined in this volume, such as youth violence or substance use. Factors at multiple levels of the ecology (individual, family, school, neighborhood) can influence a youth's progression toward school success or failure (Bronfenbrenner & Morris, 1998). To understand the etiology of early school leaving and failure, we must take a multidisciplinary approach.

General deviance theory suggests that students who are involved in drug use, alcohol abuse, or other deviant behavior are more likely to drop out of school (Battin-Pearson et al., 2000). Similarly, deviant affiliation theory posits that peers' beliefs about school and academic achievement influence their friends' behavior and attitudes (Gilmore, Hawkins, Day, & Catalano, 1992). Patterson, DeBaryshe, and Ramsey's transactional model of development (1989) suggests that children with early behavior problems are at risk for developing academic problems and experiencing rejection from their prosocial peers. Their lack of prosocial connections can lead them to form connections with deviant peers and in turn engage in other delinquent acts such as truancy, substance use, or possibly violent behavior.

The family and home environment have also been the focus of theoretical approaches to understanding early school leaving and school failure. Family socialization theory posits that students' academic achievement in the classroom is affected by their home environment (Battin-Pearson et al., 2000). Stressful events such as parental divorce, family conflict, and loss of a loved one can influence how a student behaves in and outside the classroom. In addition, parents' education level and the importance parents place on academic success can affect a student's sense of purpose and agency in the school environment. Finally, cumulative risk theory posits an inverse association between the number of risk factors and positive adjustment and acknowledges the significance of risk factors across ecological levels (Bronfenbrenner & Morris, 1998; Rutter, 1989).

Taken together, the theoretical work on early school leaving and school failure indicates that these issues are complex, that there are multiple pathways to dropout and school failure, and that a variety of factors at different ecological levels influence these processes (Ensminger & Slusarcick, 1992; Jimerson, Egeland, Sroufe, & Carlson, 2000).

Linking the Core Competencies with School Failure and Early School Leaving

There is empirical and theoretical evidence that each of the five core competencies is associated directly or indirectly with school success. The relevant contribution of each competency, however, may vary based on the developmental period. For example, the ability to self-regulate emotions and behaviors may influence early disengagement from school, whereas connections to deviant peers may have a relatively greater impact during adolescence. Given that school disengagement is a process, the interplay of these competencies over time is an essential consideration. The relevance of intellectual abilities, learning disabilities, and mental health problems should not be underestimated, as youth with these challenges are at increased risk for experiencing problems at school (Battin-Pearson et al., 2000).

Contextual factors at the level of the peer group, family, school, neighborhood, and the physical environment, such as lead exposure or social disorder, should also be considered as possibly moderating the influence of these five competencies on school success. Although there is evidence that the core competencies are important to adolescent development across cultural contexts (Barber, 2005), little research has documented whether particular competencies are more relevant in some settings than others. What is known is that the socializing behaviors that foster the core competencies vary across cultural contexts, highlighting the importance of making preventive interventions culturally relevant (McNeely & Barber, 2008).

A Positive Sense of Self. One of the mostly widely cited theories regarding school failure and dropout is the frustration–self-esteem model, which posits that poor performance leads to frustration and lower self-esteem, which in turn leads to dropout (Finn & Rock, 1997). Consequently, students who experience academic failures may develop a poor sense of self, which can put them at increased risk for other behavior problems, including delinquency and substance use. In contrast, having a positive sense of self, purpose, and efficacy has been linked with academic success (Finn & Rock, 1997). Related to these views of self are high expectations for the self, a sense of mastery regarding learning, having future aspirations, and setting academic goals (Harter, Bresnick, Bouchey, & Whitesell, 1997). Without a positive sense of self, youth are unlikely to identify extrinsic (potential earnings) and intrinsic (liking school) motivations for being successful in school (Vallerand, Fortier, & Guay, 1997). It should be noted, however, that a positive view of self in isolation is likely not sufficient for school success. In fact, the research is mixed regarding the association between self-esteem and other behavioral outcomes, such as aggression (Baumeister, Campbell, Krueger, & Vohs, 2003).

Self-Control. Several aspects of self-control, including self-regulation, impulse control, and delay of gratification, are critical for success at school. One of the most influential studies of self-control was conducted by Mischel, Shoda, and Rodriguez (1989), who explored the link between self-regulatory skills, such as the ability to delay gratification, and a range of outcomes across multiple contexts. Children who are able to exert self-control and willpower during temptation are more likely to persist when faced with obstacles. This type of self-regulation requires the child to refrain from succumbing to emotional instincts and instead cognitively focus on future gratification. Youth who are able to exert more self-control during situations of temptation typically are more academically successful, have better planning and goal-setting abilities, have more positive social-emotional functioning, and show better behavioral adjustment (Mischel & Ayduk, 2002). Although few studies have examined this paradigm with high school dropouts, it seems plausible that students who drop out of school likely have poor self-regulatory behavior and fail to consider the benefits of having a high school diploma. Youths' ability to control their impulsive behavior also likely plays a role in their ability to focus and persist when completing educational tasks. In contrast, children who are overly inhibited are disinclined to participate in class discussions, engage in classroom or school activities, and initiate social interactions with teachers and other students (Finn & Rock, 1997).

The literature on children's control beliefs suggests that perceptions of control over academic outcomes are associated with academic achievement. Conversely, students who perceive limited control over the school environment are at an increased risk of failing (Skinner, Zimmer-Gembeck, Connell, Eccles, & Wellborn, 1998). The literature on students' locus of control has produced similar results, such that students who have a high internal locus of control (they believe they control the outcome) are more likely to be successful academically, as opposed to youth who have a higher external locus of control (they believe the environment controls the outcome) (Wentzel & Wigfield, 1998). Longitudinal research on elementary school youth suggests that students' perceived control of academic engagement is related to their perceptions of teachers' supportiveness and, consequently, their academic outcomes (Skinner et al., 1998). Specifically, youth who perceived their teachers to be supportive and caring were more likely to perceive that they had control over their academic outcomes, which resulted in increased success at school.

Decision-Making Skills. School failure and dropout are a dynamic set of processes that unfold over time and thus are rarely discrete decisions. Yet a variety of decision-making skills are relevant to this dynamic process. The theory of planned behavior suggests that students' behavior is influenced by their attitudes toward the behavior, subjective norms, and perceived behavioral control, all of which affect their intention of attending school, involvement in school activities, and staying in school (Davis, Ajzen, Saunders, & Williams, 2002). Students who have high perceived behavioral control (for example, a perceived ability to succeed academically) and a positive attitude toward graduating (they understand it prepares them for work or provides a sense of accomplishment, for example) are more likely to have increased intentions of graduating and are significantly more likely to receive their high school diploma (Davis et al., 2002).

Youth who leave school early tend to have lower expectations of the rewards associated with graduating than do high school graduates (Eckstein & Wolpin, 1999), which illustrates a potential link between decision making and the delay of gratification. Other decision-making skills, such as social-emotional problem solving, maturity of judgment, relationship skills, and responsible decisions about studying and completing assignments, have been linked with achievement (Zins, Weissberg, Wang, & Walberg, 2004) and high school completion (Hawkins, Catalano, Kosterman, Abbott, & Hill, 1999). These subjective values and latent beliefs, coupled with motivational factors, can potentially influence the way in which youth make decisions related to academics.

A Moral System of Belief. A small body of research highlights the importance of empathy and social perspective taking in school success. For example, Caprara, Barbaranelli, Pastorelli, Bandura, and Zimbardo (2000) found that students' prosocial behavior, such as helpfulness, sharing, kindness, and cooperativeness, was directly related to academic achievement. Similarly, students who are more cooperative and empathetic have better academic performance (Wentzel & Wigfield, 1998). Concern for others can influence how one interacts with peers and resolves interpersonal conflict (Bradshaw & Garbarino, 2004). The more youth take a socially responsible role inside and outside the classroom, the less likely they are to become involved in such deviant behavior as drug use, early sexual activity, or alcohol abuse, which in turn reduces their likelihood of dropping out of school (Battin-Pearson et al., 2000; Garnier et al., 1997). Overall it appears that students who conform to school rules tend to perform better in the classroom setting and are less likely to leave school early.

Prosocial Connectedness. Connection to parents has a positive influence on multiple aspects of youth development. Attachment theory suggests that children's attachment to parental figures greatly affects how they interact in new situations, adapt to challenges, and interact with other people (Bowlby, 1969). Secure attachments are hypothesized to lay the foundations for a positive sense of self and view of others, which influence social cognitive factors and emotion regulation skills (Bradshaw & Garbarino, 2004). In addition to these basic attachment experiences, parents' involvement and engagement in their child's personal and academic life have been shown to promote academic achievement and school attendance (Hoover-Dempsey et al., 2005). Parents who serve as educational role models and set clear and consistent educational expectations are likely to foster a strong commitment to education in their children.

An important but often overlooked factor in children's success in school is their social connectedness to school. Social connections to teachers are negatively associated with grade repetition, suspension, and early school leaving (Catalano, Haggerty, Oesterle, Fleming, & Hawkins, 2004; Klem & Connell, 2004), as well as health-compromising behaviors such as drug use (McNeely & Falci, 2004). Teachers' caring behavior has also been shown to promote prosocial beliefs in students and motivate them to perform well in the classroom (Marcus & Sanders-Reio, 2001; Wentzel & Wigfield, 1998).

Prosocial bonds with adults at school can exert informal social control, thereby discouraging negative behaviors as well as encouraging positive ones (Catalano et al., 2004). Disorder within the school environment, however, challenges the school's functioning and interferes with the bonding process (McNeely, Nonnemaker, & Blum, 2002).

Whereas social connections to teachers consistently protect against school failure, social connections with peers can exert both positive and negative influences, depending on the characteristics of those peers. Students with friends who hold positive attitudes toward school tend to have fewer academic problems than those whose friends are less academically oriented (Crosnoe, Cavanagh, & Elder 2003). Less academically oriented students appear to be more vulnerable to the negative influences of delinquent friends, which may result from reduced acceptance of the norms of academic achievement and conventional institutions (Crosnoe, 2002).

Role of Core Competencies in Dropout and School Failure Prevention

Although in this chapter we focus on individual core competencies, they alone are not sufficient to promote school success. School dropout and failure are the end result of a cumulative process that depends not only on a youth's competencies but also on specific actions and choices of parents, caregivers, and school personnel, as well as the prevailing policies and availability of programs to support the youth. While there is ample evidence that an individual's core competencies promote school success, they can only do so when the adults in the adolescent's life provide the opportunity for educational success. Investing in or promoting a single competency will not sufficiently ameliorate the problem of school failure and dropout; rather, several competencies should be considered and targeted jointly. We now consider programs and policies showing promise in promoting success in school and high school completion.

Although there has been considerable research on the correlates of school dropout, relatively few studies have examined the effectiveness of dropout prevention programs (Prevatt & Kelly, 2003). Mentoring programs lasting at least a year, such as those following the Big Brothers/Big Sisters of America model, have been shown to reduce behavioral problems, improve social skills, and promote positive student-teacher relations (McGill, Mihalic, & Grotpeter, 1998). These effects likely occur through positive relationships and connections that are formed with adult mentors, as well as the positive role the mentor plays in the child's life (Jekielek, Moore, & Hair, 2002). Another notable educationally oriented mentoring program is Check & Connect (Evelo, Sinclair, Hurley, Christenson, & Thurlow, 1996), which aims to increase student engagement, attendance, and participation by assigning youth a school-based mentor who works with the student and family to promote effective problem solving. The program targets several of the core competencies such as promoting positive adult-youth relationships, a positive connection between the youth and school, and effective decision-making skills, along with monitoring of the child's school attendance and accomplishment of individually tailored academic goals. Evaluations of Check & Connect with at-risk students have shown that it significantly increased student attendance and engagement in the school setting (Lehr, Sinclair, & Christenson, 2004). A similar model, the Behavior Education Program, or "Check-In/Check-Out" (Crone, Horner, & Hawken, 2004), forms a positive partnership between the youth and a school staff member to create a point card that the child uses to self-monitor daily behavioral goals. This model has been shown to reduce office discipline referrals among at-risk elementary and middle school students, which likely translates into improved academic achievement (Filter et al., 2007).

Several prevention programs stress early intervention as a means of increasing academic engagement and performance. The High/Scope Perry Preschool Program, which provides early childhood education to disadvantaged children to advance their academic and eventual career performance, has been shown to reduce dropout rates and promote school commitment and favorable attitudes toward the school environment. Longitudinal studies have shown that children enrolled in the program had higher annual earnings in adulthood than controls did (Schweinhart et al., 2005). The Parent-Child Home Program is a similar prevention model that provides education and family support services to at-risk, low-income families (Levenstein, Levenstein, Shiminski, & Stolzberg, 1998). The program has been shown to reduce dropout rates, most likely by improving decision-making skills and connectedness to parents (Levenstein et al., 1998). Social-emotional programs for elementary school children, such as Promoting Alternative Thinking Strategies (Greenberg, Kusché, & Mihalic, 1998) and Second Step (Grossman et al., 1997), as well as compressive multicomponent programs like Fast Track (Bierman et al., 1999) also have been shown to affect several of the core competencies, including self-control, a moral belief system, and decision-making skills, as well as co-occurring behavioral problems. These effects likely translate into improved academic achievement and reduced school dropout.

Several dropout prevention programs aim to promote effective decision making, self-control skills, and prosocial connections. Talent Search provides low-income high school students academic mentoring, career development coaching, college campus visits, and financial aid application assistance, coupled with academic tutoring and training on test taking and study skills. Talent Search has been shown to increase high school completion (Constantine, Seftor, Martin, Silva, & Myers, 2006). Another career-focused prevention program is Career Academies, which targets at-risk high school students and combines academics with on-the-job technical training to enrich the learning process. The program establishes outside partnerships with local employers to increase the opportunities available to students and increase students' prosocial connectedness to members of the work community. The model has been shown to reduce dropout rates among high-risk youth (Kemple & Snipes, 2000).

Despite the growing interest in school connectedness, there has been relatively limited systematic research on schoolwide interventions that aim to promote students' connectedness to the school, other students, and teachers. One such schoolwide model is Positive Behavioral Interventions and Supports (PBIS), which applies social learning, behavioral, and organizational principles to promote decision-making skills, self-control, and positive connections between students and staff. Recent research indicates that PBIS improves schools' organizational environment (Bradshaw, Koth, Bevans, Ialongo, & Leaf, in press) and reduces behavior problems (Horner et al., in press), which likely translate into increased academic performance and a reduction in dropout rates. Related work by Pianta (2006) focuses on effective classroom management as a strategy for promoting positive connections between teachers and students and academic engagement.

A number of federal and state policies have been enacted to address school failure and early school leaving. The Individuals with Disabilities in Education Act and the No Child Left Behind (NCLB) act hold schools accountable for increasing academic performance and creating a safe and orderly learning environment (Rumberger & Palardy, 2005). Although there appear to be some gains in academic achievement since the passage of NCLB, the dropout rate has not wavered much during this time, particularly among urban and minority students, the highest-risk youth (Perie, Grigg, & Donahue, 2005). Several states have increased the age for compulsory education, with twenty-six states requiring students to attend school until age sixteen, nine states until age seventeen, and fifteen states until age eighteen (National Conference of State Legislatures, 2008). Despite this trend toward increasing the compulsory education age, there is little evidence that raising the age has a significant impact on dropout. Although these policies increase accountability at the school level, struggling students will likely continue to drop out if preventive interventions that target the core competencies are not in place. Consequently, it is in the great interest of schools to promote the core competencies because they are important mediators of improved educational outcomes for all students.

Future Directions

Despite the wealth of research on school failure and early school leaving, the research on the subject falls short in several areas. The research has primarily focused on describing risk factors rather than identifying specific protective factors and mechanisms involved in the promotive process.

Furthermore, much of the research has been cross-sectional or retrospective, examined influences at just one level (child, school, community, or family), or lacked a theoretical basis or consideration of developmental factors. Future studies should adopt a multidisciplinary perspective and use longitudinal prospective designs to identify factors at multiple levels and across different developmental time points that influence school success and high school completion.

There are also inconsistencies in definitions and policies used to measure dropout rates, thus reducing the reliability and validity of these data. The varying state compulsory education laws make cross-state comparisons and evaluations of federal policies difficult. Obtaining valid and reliable data on school dropout is also challenging because of inconsistencies among states' definitions of what constitutes a high school graduate (students who receive a standards-based diploma on time with their class versus receiving a general educational diploma), as well as problems associated with calculating graduation rates. There also is growing suspicion that dropout data may be misleading or biased due to the increased accountability at both the school and local levels (Rumberger & Palardy, 2005).

Finally, there are few theory-based interventions that target particular competencies or aim to bolster specific protective factors. As such, there is a limited knowledge base of evidence-based programs to prevent early school leaving across multiple school settings or at different points in the process of disengagement (Prevatt & Kelly, 2003). The increasing interest in nontraditional educational programs for high-risk students, such as charter schools, alternative programs, and innovation schools, holds promise as a possible strategy for meeting the needs of some at-risk youth. Several of these models promote core competencies, such as prosocial connections, self-control, and decision making (Franklin, Streeter, Kim, & Tripodi, 2007). Yet there have been few rigorous evaluations of these programs, and there are few longitudinal data documenting their long-term outcomes. A careful examination of the effect of these programs on the core competencies and the extent to which the competencies mediate programmatic effects on academic outcomes would not only clarify the role of the competencies over various developmental periods, but also advance knowledge about building and sustaining effective alternative educational programs.

In conclusion, the detrimental effects of school failure and early school leaving are well documented. There is compelling evidence that the five core competencies are related to school success; however, additional longitudinal and intervention research is needed to examine the specific process by which each competency promotes school success. Addressing the competencies, which are largely individual factors, in conjunction with factors operating at other levels of the youth's ecology holds the greatest promise in promoting success at school and preventing school failure and early school leaving.

References

Arnett, J. J. (2000). Emerging adulthood: A theory of development from the late teens through the twenties. *American Psychologist, 55*, 469–480.

Barber, B. K. (2005). Positive adolescent functioning: An assessment of measures across time and group. In K. A. Moore & L. Lippman (Eds.), *What do children need to flourish? Conceptualizing and measuring indicators of positive development.* New York: Springer.

Battin-Pearson, S., Newcomb, M. D., Abbott, R. D., Hill, K. G., Catalano, R. F., & Hawkins, J. D. (2000). Predictors of early high school dropout: A test of five theories. *Journal of Educational Psychology, 92*, 568–582.

Baumeister, R. F., Campbell, J. D., Krueger, J. I., & Vohs, K. D. (2003). Does high self-esteem cause better performance, interpersonal success, happiness, or healthier lifestyles? *Psychological Science in the Public Interest, 4*, 1–44.

Bierman, K. L., Coie, J. D., Dodge, K. A., Greenberg, M. T., Lochman, J. E., McMahon, R. J., et al. (1999). Initial impact of the Fast Track prevention trial for conduct problems: I. The high-risk sample. *Journal of Consulting and Clinical Psychology, 67*, 631–347.

Bowlby, J. (1969). *Attachment and loss: Vol. 1. Attachment.* New York: Basic Books.

Bradshaw, C. P., & Garbarino, J. (2004). Social cognition as a mediator of the influence of family and community violence on adolescent development: Implications for intervention. *Annuals New York Academy of Science, 1036*, 85–105.

Bradshaw, C. P., Koth, C. W., Bevans, K. B., Ialongo, N., & Leaf, P. J. (in press). The impact of school-wide positive behavioral interventions and supports (PBIS) on the organizational health of elementary schools. *School Psychology Quarterly.*

Bronfenbrenner, U., & Morris, P. (1998). The ecology of developmental processes. In W. Damon (Ed.), *Handbook of child psychology, Vol. 1. Theoretical models of human development* (pp. 993–1028). Hoboken, NJ: Wiley.

Caprara, G. V., Barbaranelli, C., Pastorelli, C., Bandura, A., & Zimbardo, P. G. (2000). Prosocial foundations of children's academic achievement. *Psychology Science, 11*, 302–306.

Catalano, R. F., Haggerty, K. P., Oesterle, S., Fleming, C. B., & Hawkins, J. (2004). The importance of bonding to school for healthy development: Findings from the Social Development Research Group. *Journal of School Health, 74*, 252–261.

Constantine, J. M., Seftor, N. S., Martin, E. S., Silva, T., & Myers, D. (2006). *A study of the effect of the Talent Search program on secondary and postsecondary outcomes in Florida, Indiana, and Texas: Final report from phase II of the national evaluation.* Washington, DC: U.S. Department of Education.

Crone, D. A., Horner, R. H., & Hawken, L. S. (2004). *Responding to problem behavior in schools: The Behavior Education Program (practical interventions in the schools).* New York: Guilford Press.

Crosnoe, R. (2002). High school curriculum track and adolescent association with delinquent friends. *Journal of Adolescent Research, 17*, 143–167.

Crosnoe, R., Cavanagh, S., & Elder, G. H. (2003) Adolescent friendships as academic resources: The intersection of friendship, race, and school disadvantage. *Sociological Perspectives, 46*, 331–352.

Davis, L. E., Ajzen, I., Saunders, J., & Williams, T. (2002). The decision of African American students to complete high school: An application of the theory of planned behavior. *Journal of Educational Psychology, 94*, 810–819.

Eckstein, Z., & Wolpin, K. I. (1999). Why youth drop out of high school: The impact of preferences, opportunities, and abilities. *Econometrica, 67*, 1295–1339.

Ensminger, M. E., & Slusarcick, A. L. (1992). Paths to high school graduation or dropout: A longitudinal study of a first grade cohort. *Sociology of Education, 65*, 95–113.

Evelo, D., Sinclair, M., Hurley, C., Christenson, S., & Thurlow, M. (1996). *Keeping kids in school: Using Check and Connect for dropout prevention.* Minneapolis: University of Minnesota, Institute on Community Integration.

Filter, K. J., McKenna, M. K., Benedict, E. A., Horner, R. H., Todd, A. W., & Watson, J. (2007). Check in/check out: A post-hoc evaluation of an efficient, secondary level targeted intervention for reducing problem behaviors in schools. *Education and Treatment of Children, 30,* 69–84.

Finn, J. D., & Rock, D. A. (1997). Academic success among students at risk for school failure. *Journal of Applied Psychology, 82,* 221–234.

Franklin, C., Streeter, C. L., Kim, J. S., & Tripodi, S. J. (2007). The effectiveness of a solution-focused, public alternative school for dropout prevention and retrieval. *Children and Schools, 29,* 133–144.

French, D. C., & Conrad, J. (2001). School dropout as predicted by peer rejection and antisocial behavior. *Journal of Research on Adolescence, 11,* 225–244.

Garnier, H. E., Stein, J. A., & Jacobs, J. K. (1997). The process of dropping out of high school: A 19-year perspective. *American Educational Research Journal, 34,* 395–419.

Gilmore, M. R., Hawkins, J. D., Day, L. E., & Catalano, R. F. (1992). Friendship and deviance: New evidence on an old controversy. *Journal of Early Adolescence, 12,* 80–95.

Greenberg, M. T., Kusché, C., & Mihalic, S. F. (1998). *Promoting Alternative Thinking Strategies (PATHS): Blueprints for violence prevention, Book Ten.* Boulder, CO: Institute of Behavioral Science.

Grossman, D. C., Neckerman, H. J., & Koepsell, T. D, Liu, P. Y., Asher, K. N., Beland, K., et al. (1997). The effectiveness of a violence prevention curriculum among children in elementary school: A randomized controlled trial. *JAMA, 277,* 1605–1611.

Harter, S., Bresnick, S., Bouchey, H., & Whitesell, N. R. (1997). The development of multiple role-related selves in adolescence. *Development and Psychopathology, 9,* 835–854.

Hawkins, J. D., Catalano, R. F., Kosterman, R., Abbott, R., & Hill, K. G. (1999). Preventing adolescent health-risk behaviors by strengthening protection during childhood. *Archives of Pediatric Adolescent Medicine, 153,* 226–234.

Hoover-Dempsey, K. V., Walker, J.M.T., Sandler, H. M., Whetsel, D., Green, C. L., Wilkins, A. S., et al. (2005). Why do parents become involved? Research findings and implications. *Elementary School Journal, 106,* 105–131.

Horner, R. H., Sugai, G., Smolkowski, K., Eber, L., Nakasato, J., Todd, A. W., et al. (in press). A randomized, wait-list controlled effectiveness trial assessing school-wide positive behavior support in elementary schools. *Journal of Positive Behavior Interventions.*

Institute of Education Sciences. (2008). *Fast facts.* Retrieved September 2, 2008, from http://nces.ed.gov/fastfacts/display.asp?id=16.

Jekielek, S., Moore, K. A., & Hair, E. (2002). *Mentoring programs and youth development: A synthesis.* Washington, DC: Child Trends.

Jimerson, S. R., Egeland, B., Sroufe, L. A., & Carlson, B. (2000). A prospective longitudinal study of high school dropouts: Examining multiple predictors across development. *Journal of School Psychology, 38,* 525–549.

Kemple, J. J., & Snipes, J. C. (2000). *Career academies: Impacts on students' engagement and performance in high school.* New York: Manpower Demonstration Research Corporation.

Klem, A. M., & Connell, J. P. (2004). Relationships matter: Linking teacher support to student engagement and achievement. *Journal of School Health, 74,* 262–273.

Lehr, C. A., Sinclair, M. F., & Christenson, S. L. (2004). Addressing student engagement and truancy prevention during the elementary school years: A replication study of the Check and Connect model. *Journal of Education for Students Placed at Risk, 9,* 279–301.

Levenstein, P., Levenstein, S., Shiminski, J. A., & Stolzberg, J. E. (1998). Long-term impact of a verbal interaction program for at-risk toddlers: An exploratory study of high school outcomes in a replication of the Mother-Child Home Program. *Journal of Applied Developmental Psychology, 19,* 267–286.

Lochner, L., & Moretti, E. (2004). The effect of education on crime: Evidence from prison inmates, arrests, and self reports. *American Economic Review, 94,* 155–189.

Marcus, R. F., & Sanders-Reio, J. (2001). The influence of attachment on school completion. *School Psychology Quarterly, 16*, 427–444.

McGill, D. E., Mihalic, S. F., & Grotpeter, J. K. (1998). *Blueprints for violence prevention, Book Two: Big Brothers Big Sisters of America*. Boulder, CO: Center for the Study and Prevention of Violence.

McNeely, C. A., & Barber, B. K. (2008). *How do parents make adolescents feel loved? The perspective of adolescents from 12 cultures*. Unpublished manuscript.

McNeely, C. A., & Falci, C. (2004). School connectedness and the transition into and out of health-risk behavior among adolescents: A comparison of social belonging and teacher support. *Journal of School Health, 74*, 284–292.

McNeely, C. A., Nonnemaker, J. M., & Blum, R. W. (2002). Promoting school connectedness: Evidence from the national longitudinal study of adolescent health. *Journal of School Health, 72*, 138–146.

Mischel, W., & Ayduk, O. (2002). Self-regulation in a cognitive-affective personality system: Attentional control in the service of the self. *Self and Identity, 1*, 113–120.

Mischel, W., Shoda, Y., & Rodriguez, M. (1989). Delay of gratification in children. *Science, 244*, 933–938.

National Conference of State Legislatures. (2008). *Compulsory education: Legislation and laws 2005*. Retrieved February 13, 2008, from http://www.ncsl.org/programs/educ/CompulsoryEdLegislation.htm.

Newcomb, M. D., Abbott, R. D., Catalano, R. F., Hawkins, J. D., Battin-Pearson, S., & Hill, K. (2002). Mediational and deviance theories of late high school failure: Process roles of structural strains, academic competence, and general versus specific problem behaviors. *Journal of Counseling Psychology, 49*, 172–186.

Patterson, G. R., DeBaryshe, B. D., & Ramsey, E. (1989). A developmental perspective on antisocial behavior. *American Psychologist, 44*, 329–335.

Perie, M., Grigg, W. S., & Donahue, P. L. (2005). *Nation's report card: Reading 2005*. Washington, DC: U.S. Department of Education, Institute of Education Sciences.

Pianta, R. C. (2006). Classroom management and relationships between children and teachers: Implications for research and practice. In C. M. Evertson & C. S. Weinstein (Eds.), *Handbook of classroom management: Research, practice, and contemporary issues* (pp. 685–709). Mahwah, NJ: Erlbaum.

Prevatt, F., & Kelly, F. D. (2003). Dropping out of school: A review of intervention programs. *Journal of School Psychology, 41*, 377–395.

Rumberger, R. W., & Palardy, G. J. (2005). Does segregation still matter? The impact of student composition on academic achievement in high school. *Teachers College Record, 107*, 1999–2045.

Rutter, M. (1989). Pathways from childhood to adult life. *Journal of Child Psychology Psychiatry, 30*, 23–51.

Schweinhart, L. J., Montie, J., Xiang, Z., Barnett, W. S., Belfield, C. R., & Nores, M. (2005). *Lifetime effects: The High/Scope Perry Preschool Study through age 40*. Ypsilanti, MI: High/Scope Press.

Skinner, E. A., Zimmer-Gembeck, M. J., Connell, J. P., Eccles, J. S., & Wellborn, J. G. (1998). Individual differences and the development of perceived control. *Monographs of the Society for Research in Child Development, 63*, 1–220.

Vallerand, R. J., Fortier, M. S., & Guay, F. (1997). Self-determination and persistence in a real-life setting: Toward a motivational model of high school dropout. *Journal of Personality and Social Psychology, 72*, 1161–1176.

Vernez, G., Krop, R. A., & Rydell, C. P. (1999). *Closing the education gap: Benefits and costs*. Santa Monica, CA: Rand Corp.

Wentzel, K. R., & Wigfield, A. (1998). Academic and social motivational influences on students' academic performance. *Educational Psychology Review, 10*, 155–175.

Zins, J. E., Weissberg, R. P., Wang, M. C., & Walberg, H. J. (2004). *Building school success through social and emotional learning*. New York: Teachers College Press.

CATHERINE P. BRADSHAW is an assistant professor and the associate director for the Johns Hopkins Center for the Prevention of Youth Violence at the Johns Hopkins Bloomberg School of Public Health.

LINDSEY M. O'BRENNAN is a research assistant with the Johns Hopkins Center for the Prevention of Youth Violence and a doctoral student at the University of California, Santa Barbara.

CLEA A. MCNEELY is an assistant professor and the deputy director for the Adolescent Health Center at the Johns Hopkins Bloomberg School of Public Health.

Sullivan, T. N., Farrell, A. D., Bettencourt, A. F., & Helms, S. W. (2008). Core competencies and the prevention of youth violence. In N. G. Guerra & C. P. Bradshaw (Eds.), *Core competencies to prevent problem behaviors and promote positive youth development*. New Directions for Child and Adolescent Development, 122, 33–46.

3

Core Competencies and the Prevention of Youth Violence

Terri N. Sullivan, Albert D. Farrell, Amie F. Bettencourt, Sarah W. Helms

Abstract

We discuss how the five core competencies for healthy adjustment in adolescence (a positive sense of self, self-control, decision-making skills, a moral system of belief, and prosocial connectedness) are represented in theories of aggression and youth violence. We then discuss research supporting the relation between these core competencies and aggressive and violent behavior in childhood and adolescence. Finally, we address the degree to which these core competencies have been included and systematically evaluated within school-based prevention programs, and we end with suggestions for future directions. © Wiley Periodicals, Inc.

Youth violence is a serious public health concern: it is the second leading cause of fatal injuries for adolescents, and over 300,000 youth were treated in emergency departments in 2006 for nonfatal injuries resulting from violence (Centers for Disease Control and Prevention, 2008). Prevalence rates for violence-related behaviors are particularly high among adolescents. A national sample of U.S. high school students indicated that 36 percent had engaged in a physical fight in the past year and 19 percent had carried a weapon in the past thirty days (Centers for Disease Control and Prevention, 2005).

These high rates of violence and violence-related behaviors have serious consequences for both victims and perpetrators. Victimization and witnessing violence are linked to increased internalizing and externalizing behaviors among children and adolescents (Juvonen & Graham, 2001). Youth violence also is related to negative consequences for perpetrators in a number of areas, including peer relationships, academic achievement, and arrest outcomes, and it is highly related to other risk-taking behaviors such as substance use, delinquency, and risky sexual behavior (Pepler, Madsen, Webster, & Levene, 2005).

This chapter links youth violence prevention with the promotion of the five core competencies for healthy adjustment in adolescence (a positive sense of self, self-control, decision-making skills, a moral system of belief, and prosocial connectedness) outlined in the first chapter of this volume. To the extent that youth violence is linked to other risk-taking behaviors (Pepler et al., 2005), it is important to highlight these common predictors. We begin with an overview of some guiding theories, summarize research indicating an association between the core competencies and youth violence, and conclude with a brief summary of evidence-based violence prevention strategies that incorporate the core competencies. In many cases, we build on theoretical and empirical work in childhood aggression given the robust connection between early childhood aggression and youth violence (Moffitt, 1993).

Theoretical Perspectives on Youth Violence

The complex nature of youth violence has led to a multitude of theories to explain its nature, prevalence, and etiology. No single theory can adequately account for youth violence in all its various forms (Tolan & Guerra, 1994). Several theories emphasize differences in the developmental trajectories associated with violence and antisocial behavior (Moffitt, 1993). Others, such as social-cognitive information processing (SCIP) theories (Crick & Dodge, 1994; Huesmann, 1998), focus on the role of beliefs about aggression and cognitive processes that lead to aggressive behavior, with some empirical support linking these processes with aggression and violence during adolescence (Tolan & Guerra, 1994).

The social development model emphasizes individual competencies and skills as embedded in social contexts. Positive attachment with others in combination with prosocial values is seen as important for the prevention of problem behaviors such as aggression and delinquency (Hawkins, Catalano, Morrison, O'Donnell, Abbott, & Day, 1992). Broader contextual models such as Bronfenbrenner's socioecological model (1997) and Lerner's developmental contextual model (Lerner & Castellino, 2002) provide a template to explore how connections between youth and family, friends, peers, and other adults in various contexts help adolescents cope adaptively with high-risk situations and may reduce their risk for involvement in violence. These developmental, social-cognitive, and contextual theories have had a significant influence on contemporary research on the etiology and prevention of childhood aggression and youth violence, serving as a foundation for many evidence-based preventive intervention strategies.

Linking the Core Competencies with Youth Violence

This section provides an overview of research relating the five core competencies to youth violence. Because of the strong influence of SCIP models on aggression research, they provide the framework for much of this discussion. However, relevant research focusing on other theoretical perspectives is also included. It is important to note that most of the research on youth violence operates from a risk rather than a strengths perspective. Specifically, youth with deficits in specific competencies are viewed as having a higher risk for engagement in violence. This emphasis is largely due to a research base that focuses on comparing aggressive or violent youth to their nonaggressive counterparts. Because nonaggressive youth are a heterogeneous group, this approach may not identify factors associated with positive adjustment (Farrell, Erwin, Mays, Bettencourt et al., 2008). As an example, among eight patterns of adjustment for victimized youth identified by Hanish and Guerra (2002), some represented maladjustment encompassing primarily internalizing symptoms.

A Positive Sense of Self. Research on SCIP has identified important differences in the self-schemas of aggressive and nonaggressive youth, including variations in self-efficacy, or the perception of one's ability to enact specific behaviors. For example, Crick and Dodge (1994) noted that youth may be more likely to enact an aggressive response if they are more confident in their ability to fight than to walk away from a provocation. In contrast, youth who are confident in their ability to use prosocial responses are less likely to make an aggressive response (Ludwig & Pittman, 1999).

As noted elsewhere in this volume, adolescents' behavior may be motivated by opportunities to enhance their self-esteem in particular domains. This can increase the likelihood of aggressive behavior for some youth and decrease it for others depending on their goals and values. Fagan and Wilkinson (1998) argued that violence can play a critical role in establishing and perpetuating an individual's self-image, particularly for males in inner-city environments, where a tough image is often related to achieving status. The value placed on maintaining this image is reinforced by peer and broader media influences (Anderson et al., 2003; Losel, Bliesener, & Bender, 2007). Qualitative work by Farrell, Erwin, Mays et al. (2008) supports this notion and suggests that many adolescents experience pressure to fight in response to peer provocation in order to avoid damaging their status with peers. In contrast, youth with a more prosocial self-image are able to avoid such pressure and are more likely to engage in prosocial behaviors. Few studies, however, consider how processes of identity development may be related to risk-taking behavior such as youth violence. A notable exception is research examining the role of ethnic identity as a protective factor that may mitigate involvement in violence and the inclusion of components focused on positive ethnic identity development in some violence prevention programs (Guerra & Smith, 2005).

Self-Control. Low self-control, including both emotional and behavioral regulation, exerts an important influence on aggressive behavior in childhood and adolescence (Finkenauer, Engels, & Baumeister, 2005). Emotion regulation, at a broad level, refers to emotion as a behavior regulator and a regulated phenomenon (Campos, Frankel, & Camras, 2004). The relation between poor emotion regulation and aggression is well documented (Orobio de Castro, Merk, Koops, Veerman, & Bosch, 2005). Behavior regulation reflects the ability to control impulses and respond to stimuli in a controlled manner (Cooper, Wood, Orcutt, & Albino, 2003), and it may be influenced by emotion regulation and executive functioning abilities. Although less well researched than emotion regulation, several studies have identified relations between poor behavior regulation, including impulsivity and reactive control, executive functioning, and externalizing behavior problems (Cooper et al., 2003).

The influence of both emotional and behavior regulation depends in part on the specific type of aggressive or violent behavior. As SCIP theories have emphasized, instrumental forms of aggression require some planning in service of social and material goals; these behaviors require controlled processing and at least some degree of self-control. In contrast, reactive aggression is manifested in impulsive reactions to provocation and is linked more clearly to poor emotional and behavior regulation (Crick & Dodge, 1994; Lemerise & Arsenio, 2000). These distinctions provide an important framework for discussing aspects of SCIP related to self-control (Fontaine, 2006).

Emotion regulation processes are apparent within SCIP models in that recognition and encoding of cues in social situations encompass emotional arousal; this arousal in turn influences how such situations are interpreted and goals prioritized to deal with them. In accessing and deciding on a response, children and adolescents may consider their emotional reaction to a potential response and also the probable emotional reaction of others (Crick & Dodge, 1994). Reactive aggressive youth who are less able to control negative emotions such as anger may struggle with initial stages of social information processing, being more likely to display a hostile attribution bias when interpreting the intent of social cues and having difficulty generating a range of potential responses to these cues (Dodge & Schwartz, 1997).

Gottfredson (2007) put forth a more ecological perspective on the role of self-control in youth violence and delinquency. According to self-control theory, not only are low levels of individual self-regulation related to criminal behavior, but specific developmental contexts can activate and motivate this self-control. In other words, although individuals can attain self-serving goals through violent behavior, positive socialization by friends, family, and other adults can also prevent violence by motivating self-control (Gottfredson, 2007).

Decision-Making Skills. Deficits in decision-making processes are central to SCIP theories. Aggressive and nonaggressive adolescents have been found to differ in processes that determine the information and goals on which a decision is based and in specific decision-making steps. Other core competencies, including positive sense of self, self-control, and a moral system of belief, also influence individual decision-making processes. Aggressive youth (that is, reactive aggressors) may reach a decision-making point in social situations with different information and goals than nonaggressive youth based on biases in information processing, including selectively attending to negative social cues, attributing hostile intent to these cues, and prioritizing revenge-based versus prosocial goals in addressing these situations (Crick & Dodge, 1994; Fontaine, 2006).

Fontaine and Dodge (2006) outlined the important role of key processes during the response evaluation and decision phase of SCIP models, including response acceptability, evaluating potential responses and outcomes expected, and response selection. They also note how decision-making steps are linked to skills and beliefs that reflect many of the core competencies, for instance, self-control, self schema, and a moral system of belief. As an example, low self-control in terms of emotional reactivity and impulsivity has been associated with poor decision making, resulting in risk-taking behavior (Cooper et al., 2003). This may be due in part to youth circumventing the response evaluation and decision phase altogether and relying more heavily on preexisting cognitive schemas and scripts (Fontaine & Dodge, 2006).

The SCIP model evaluating response acceptability also encompasses aspects of a positive sense of self (for example, adolescents with nonviolent self-concepts may be unlikely to view violent responses as acceptable), more general sociomoral decisions such as the potential harmful nature of a response, and the context of specific social situations (Fontaine & Dodge, 2006). Nelson and Crick (1999) found that compared to their peers, prosocial youth were less likely to exhibit hostile attribution bias in potential conflict situations, view aggressive responses as acceptable, and believe that aggressive responses will lead to favorable outcomes, and were more likely to value prosocial responses in such situations. In contrast, aggressive youth were less likely to engage in these patterns of behavior and had a greater likelihood than nonaggressive youth of selecting and enacting aggressive responses (Crick & Dodge, 1994).

A Moral System of Belief. Strong theoretical and empirical support links moral beliefs and aggression. Stage theories of moral development (Kohlberg & Kramer, 1969) provide important conceptual underpinnings for more recent literature emphasizing the links between social reasoning and aggression. In particular, the domain model of moral development differentiates aspects of the child's sociomoral world that are moral and nonmoral based on concepts of fairness, justice, and conventional rules (Turiel, 1989). The integration of this model into Crick and Dodge's SCIP model (1994) provides a framework for understanding both reactive and proactive aggression through specifying the influence of latent mental structures reflecting underlying conceptions about moral versus nonmoral boundaries, the acceptability of aggression (normative beliefs supporting aggression), and processing steps that may or may not involve consideration of sociomoral concerns (such as intention to harm) in deciding how to respond in a given situation (Arsenio & Lemerise, 2004; Guerra, Nucci, & Huesmann, 1994; Huesmann & Guerra, 1997). Although some measurement concerns exist in empirical evaluation of such a model, it provides important directions for future study on SCIP, moral development, and aggression (Dodge & Rabiner, 2004).

In addition to SCIP approaches to the role of a moral system of belief in aggression and violence, related constructs such as empathy and callous/unemotional personality traits have been linked with aggression. Specifically, callous/unemotional traits, which reflect lack of concern about moral considerations and difficulty with empathy, have been found to be related to aggression (Pardini, Lochman, & Frick, 2003). Also, a number of studies highlight relations between empathy-related responding (both dispositional and situation specific) and prosocial behavior among youth (Eisenberg, 2002).

Prosocial Connectedness. The inverse relation between prosocial connectedness and aggression is supported by studies demonstrating the protective role of secure attachment and family support (Malecki & Demaray, 2004). For caregiver-child relationships, research on attachment theory highlights prosocial outcomes stemming from secure attachment in associated self-regulation, empathic, moral, and emotional development from infancy through adulthood (Gauthier, 2003; van Ijzendoorn, 1997). There is empirical support to suggest that in late adolescence and emerging adulthood, self-esteem may partially mediate the effect of parental attachment on aggression and moderate the relation between maternal attachment and aggression (Gomez & McLaren, 2007). Broadening this perspective to encompass peer influences, evidence suggests that adolescents with strong parent and peer attachments are less aggressive than youth with low attachment in either the peer or parent domain, with the highest levels of aggression displayed among youth with low parent and peer attachment (Laible, Carlo, & Raffaelli, 2000).

Other work documents the impact of prosocial connectedness to broader social institutions such as schools, neighborhoods, and communities. School bonding is positively associated with school adjustment and perceived school climate and negatively related to problem behaviors, including violence (Catalano, Haggerty, Oesterle, Fleming, & Hawkins, 2004). Developmental-ecological models of violence suggest that examination of prosocial connectedness at a macrosystem level may be important in understanding youth violence. Constructs such as community structure (for example, concentration of poverty, economic resources, and violent crime rates) and neighborhood social organization may relate to youth violence (Tolan, Gorman-Smith, & Henry, 2003). However, microsystem connections such as family relationship characteristics may exert a protective influence even for youth at risk of violence perpetration due to community-level factors (Gorman-Smith, Henry, & Tolan, 2004).

Role of Core Competencies in Youth Violence Prevention

Increasing concern about youth violence has led to the development of a diverse array of prevention strategies. Schools have been the most frequent focus of violence prevention efforts because they represent a primary context for social development and provide an efficient method to reach large numbers of youths (Farrell & Camou, 2006). Because prevention programs often begin early during the preschool or elementary school years, the outcome of interest typically is aggression and acting-out behavior rather than serious violence. This section discusses the extent to which prevention strategies attempt to address the five core competencies and is organized by broad categories of prevention (universal, selective or indicated, and multilevel and multimodal programs). Within each category, general trends are illustrated by highlighting representative programs that have shown promise in preventing aggression or violence. Because evaluations of specific programs have not always produced consistent findings, interested readers should refer to the original sources for details and reviews of this complex literature (Wilson & Lipsey, 2007).

Universal Programs. Universal programs aim to prevent behavior problems by focusing on an entire population, such as all students, regardless of their level of risk (Farrell & Camou, 2006). The majority of these programs include a student curriculum, sometimes implemented with other strategies designed to promote school-level changes, such as peer mediation or teacher training (Wilson & Lipsey, 2007). Universal curricula differ in their behavioral targets, with some focused on individual or interpersonal relationships, others on changing social norms and environment, and still others on a combination of these factors (Hahn et al., 2007). Recent reviews have identified a variety of universal programs that vary in their level of effectiveness at reducing aggression (Hahn et al., 2007; Wilson & Lipsey, 2007).

The most common types of universal programs focus on modifying aggressive behavior by altering some of the core competencies (for instance, decision-making skills, consequential thinking strategies, challenging and altering moral beliefs about aggressive behavior, and developing self-efficacy for nonviolent behaviors) using affective, cognitive, and behavioral intervention strategies (Boxer & Dubow, 2002; Wilson & Lipsey, 2007). For example, Responding in Peaceful and Positive ways (RIPP; Meyer, Farrell, Northup, Kung, & Plybon, 2000) is a seven-step problem-solving process that highlights decision-making skills. RIPP improved knowledge of the problem-solving model and produced some promising effects on aggression when implemented across multiple grade levels (Farrell, Valois, Meyer, & Tidwell, 2003). Another example is Second Step (Frey, Hirschstein, & Guzzo, 2000), which bolsters self-control by teaching youth to recognize anger cues and use stress-reduction techniques to inhibit impulsive responses. Second Step has shown promising effects on empathy and anger control but mixed effects on aggression (Cooke et al., 2007; McMahon & Washburn, 2003).

Universal social skills training programs that teach youth conflict management and communication skills and promote prosocial decision-making skills and empathy (Wilson & Lipsey, 2007) have also shown promise in reducing aggression (Hahn et al., 2007). For example, the Resolving Conflict Creatively Program (RCCP), which teaches youth active listening, assertiveness, perspective taking, negotiation, and problem solving, has been found to reduce youth risk, including aggression and biased social-cognitive processing patterns. Furthermore, these effects were moderated by the number of lessons youth received and level of teacher training, with exposure to more RCCP lessons and higher levels of teacher training being associated with significant reductions in risk (Aber, Brown, & Jones, 2003). Contingency management techniques that target self-control skills, decision making, and sense of self have also shown promise in decreasing disruptive and aggressive behavior (Wilson & Lipsey, 2007). The Good Behavior Game (Kellam, Ling, Merisca, Brown, & Ialongo, 1998) uses applied behavior management strategies to help children manage their own and their teammates' maladaptive and adaptive behaviors and has been shown to decrease impulsive and disruptive behavior (Embry, 2002).

Other universal prevention programs directly targeting the school environment or climate have been found to reduce violent behavior significantly (Hahn et al., 2007). For example, PeaceBuilders (Embry, Flannery, Vazsonyi, Powell, & Atha, 1996) targets aspects of the school setting that trigger aggression and focuses on increasing prosocial models to promote change in the school climate. This intervention has produced significant improvements in youth social competence and decreased aggressive behavior (Flannery et al., 2003).

Selective and Indicated Interventions. Selective and indicated interventions represent secondary prevention efforts. Selective interventions target youth considered at high risk for aggression; indicated interventions target those already showing high levels of aggression (Farrell & Camou, 2006). Such programs reflect the fact that children at different levels of risk may benefit from interventions that vary in focus and intensity. As with universal programs, selective and indicated interventions often focus on cognitive processes but may also include social, behavioral, counseling, and peer mediation components (Wilson & Lipsey, 2007).

Cognitively oriented selective and indicated interventions have displayed promising effects on aggression. For example, a major goal of the Early Risers program is to prevent a developmental pathway toward antisocial behavior by effecting change in four core areas, one of which is behavior self-regulation (August, Realmuto, Hektner, & Bloomquist, 2001). In a recent evaluation within a sample of high-risk kindergartners, highly aggressive intervention participants evidenced greater improvements in self-regulation skills compared to highly aggressive control youth. In addition, program participants showed significant improvements in school behaviors compared to controls (August et al., 2001).

Selective and indicated interventions have also used social skills training to change aggressive behavior of high-risk youth by improving decision-making skills, empathy, and self-concept. Overall, evaluations of the effectiveness of these programs have revealed promising effects on aggression (Wilson & Lipsey, 2007). For instance, the Positive Adolescents Choices Training Program teaches youth who lack communication, negotiation, and problem-solving skills the specific social skills to improve their ability to form violence-free relationships. In an evaluation of this program, intervention youth displayed improvements in all skills training areas and decreased involvement in aggression (Hammond & Yung, 1991).

Multilevel Programs. Multilevel intervention programs include both primary and secondary prevention (that is, universal plus selective prevention). These programs have produced promising effects on aggression (Wilson & Lipsey, 2007). For example, Fast Track combines targeted and universal prevention components and intervenes at the individual, classroom, school, and family levels. The universal curriculum of Fast Track focuses on understanding and communicating emotions, developing self-control and awareness and communication of affect, and improving positive social behaviors such as communication skills, whereas the selective program provides youth social skills training groups, academic tutoring, and parent training groups. Evaluation of the combined universal and selective programs revealed positive effects on youth social cognitions, social competence, and conduct problems (Conduct Problems Prevention Research Group, 2004). A multilevel, multimodal program, the Metropolitan Area Child Study (Metropolitan Area Child Study Research Group, 2002), includes general classroom enhancement (targeting teaching practices) and the "Yes I Can" curriculum on problem solving, empathy, and beliefs supporting aggression, while the selective intervention uses family interventions and small group training to target communication, support, norms, and beliefs about aggression. This comprehensive intervention was found to reduce aggression only for younger youth living in communities with more than the minimum level of economic resources and environmental supports; however, it did not show similar effects for older elementary school youth or those youth living in inner-city communities.

Future Directions

The five core competencies highlighted in this volume play a central role in many theories of childhood aggression and youth violence, and this role has largely been supported by empirical evidence. Not surprisingly, the core competencies have also been a key focus of many violence-prevention programs. Although important progress has been made, further progress requires a more refined understanding of the link between the core competencies and violence and how best to design interventions that promote these competencies.

Much of the empirical literature has focused on the relation between the core competencies and fairly global constructs such as aggression and externalizing problems. The fact that there are multiple forms of violence that differ in their etiology and age of onset (Tolan & Guerra, 1994) suggests the need for a more refined focus that establishes the relation between core competencies and specific forms of violence. The development of effective interventions requires an understanding of the risk and protective factors most salient for the development of a particular problem within a specific subgroup and effective strategies to modify these factors (Coie et al., 1993). This underscores the need for a clearer understanding of the factors that influence the development of core competencies and how they are shaped during different stages of development for specific subgroups of youth (Boxer, Goldstein, Musher-Eizenman, Dubow, & Heretick, 2005). It also highlights the need to address these competencies within the context of a more comprehensive approach to prevention that promotes environmental changes that support changes at the individual level (Farrell, Erwin, Mays, et al., 2008).

Although basic research on core competencies can inform prevention efforts, well-designed prevention studies can enhance our understanding of core competencies by providing experimental tests of their influence on adjustment variables such as violence and other problematic outcomes (Coie et al., 1993). Unfortunately, evaluations of youth violence prevention programs have taken limited advantage of this opportunity. Few studies have included a full assessment of the risk and protective factors targeted by the intervention (Farrell & Vulin-Reynolds, 2007). Including measures of the core competencies in evaluations of violence prevention programs would provide valuable information. Such information includes the distribution of these competencies in specific populations of youth, their trajectories of change over time as represented by levels within control groups, the relation between core competencies and outcomes, the extent to which specific interventions are able to alter these processes, and the extent to which changes in the core competencies are associated with changes in outcomes. Ideally the use of common measures across studies could provide a basis for integrating this important information across studies and investigators. More generally, the inclusion of such measures in studies evaluating the impact of prevention strategies focused on different outcomes (for example, violence, drug use, risky sexual behavior) could provide a basis for identifying both commonalities and differences in the relation between competencies and specific outcomes and cross-fertilization among researchers sharing a common goal of identifying the most effective strategies for promoting this set of protective factors.

References

Aber, J. L., Brown, J. L., & Jones, S. M. (2003). Developmental trajectories toward violence in middle childhood: Course, demographic differences, and response to school-based intervention. *Developmental Psychology, 39,* 324–348.

Anderson, C. A., Berkowitz, L., Donnerstein, E., Huesmann, L. R., Johnson, J. D., Linz, D., et al. (2003). The influence of media violence on youth. *Psychological Science in the Public Interest, 4,* 81–110.

Arsenio, W. F., & Lemerise, E. A. (2004). Aggression and moral development: Integrating social information processing and moral domain models. *Child Development, 75,* 987–1002.

August, G. J., Realmuto, G. M., Hektner, J. M., & Bloomquist, M. L. (2001). An integrated components preventive intervention for aggressive elementary school children: The early risers program. *Journal of Consulting and Clinical Psychology, 69,* 614–626.

Boxer, P., & Dubow, E. F. (2002). A social-cognitive information-processing model for school-based aggression reduction and prevention programs: Issues for research and practice. *Applied and Preventive Psychology, 10,* 177–192.

Boxer, P. Goldstein, S. E., Musher-Eizenman, D., Dubow, E. F., & Heretick, D. (2005). Developmental issues in school-based aggression prevention from a social-cognitive perspective. *Journal of Primary Prevention, 26,* 383–400.

Bronfenbrenner, U. (1997). Ecological models of human development. In M. Gauvain & M. Cole (Eds.), *Readings on the development of children* (2nd ed., pp. 37–43). New York: Freeman.

Campos, J. J., Frankel, C. B., & Camras, L. (2004). On the nature of emotion regulation. *Child Development, 75,* 377–394.

Catalano, R. F., Haggerty, K. P., Oesterle, S., Fleming, C. B., & Hawkins, J. D. (2004). The importance of bonding to school for healthy development: Findings from the Social Development Research Group. *Journal of School Health, 74,* 252–261.

Centers for Disease Control and Prevention. (2005). Youth risk behavioral surveillance—United States. *Morbidity and Mortality Weekly Report, 55*(Suppl. 5), 1–112.

Centers for Disease Control and Prevention. (2008). *Web-Based Injury Statistics Query and Reporting System (WISQARS).* Retrieved January 28, 2008, from www.cdc.gov/ncipc/wisqars.

Coie, J. D., Watt, N. F., West, S. G., Hawkins, J. D., Asarnow, J. R., Markman, H. J., et al. (1993). The science of prevention: A conceptual framework and some directions for a national research program. *American Psychologist, 48,* 1013–1022.

Conduct Problems Prevention Research Group. (1999). Initial impact of the Fast Track prevention trial for conduct problems: II. Classroom effects. *Journal of Consulting and Clinical Psychology, 67,* 648–657.

Conduct Problems Prevention Research Group. (2004). The effects of the Fast Track Program on serious problem outcomes at the end of elementary school. *Journal of Clinical Child and Adolescent Psychology, 33,* 650–661.

Cooke, M. B., Ford, J., Levine, J., Bourke, C., Newell, L., & Lapidus, G. (2007). The effects of city-wide implementation of "Second Step" on elementary school students' prosocial and aggressive behaviors. *Journal of Primary Prevention, 28,* 93–115.

Cooper, M. L., Wood, P. K., Orcutt, H. K., & Albino, A. (2003). Personality and the predisposition to engage in risky or problem behaviors during adolescence. *Journal of Personality and Social Psychology, 84,* 390–410.

Crick, N., & Dodge, K. (1994). A review and reformulation of social information-processing mechanisms in children's social adjustment. *Psychological Bulletin, 115,* 74–101.

Dodge, K. A., & Rabiner, D. L. (2004). Returning to roots: On social information processing and moral development. *Child Development, 75,* 1003–1008.

Dodge, K. A., & Schwartz, D. (1997). Social information processing mechanisms in aggressive behavior. In D. Stoff, J. Breiling, & J. Maser (Eds.), *Handbook of antisocial behavior* (pp. 171–180). Hoboken, NJ: Wiley.

Eisenberg, N. (2002). Emotion, regulation, and moral development. *Annual Review in Psychology, 51,* 665–697.

Embry, D. D. (2002). The Good Behavior Game: A best practice candidate as a universal behavioral vaccine. *Clinical Child and Family Psychology Review, 5,* 273–297.

Embry, D. D., Flannery, D. J., Vazsonyi, A. T., Powell, K. E., & Atha, H. (1996). PeaceBuilders: A theoretically driven, school-based model for early violence prevention. *American Journal of Preventive Medicine, 12,* 91–100.

Fagan, J., & Wilkinson, D. L. (1998). Social contexts and functions of adolescent violence. In D. Elliott, B. Hamburg, & K. Williams (Eds.), *Violence in American schools: A new perspective* (pp. 55–93). Cambridge: Cambridge University Press.

Farrell, A. D., & Camou, S. (2006). School-based interventions for youth violence prevention. In J. Lutzker (Ed.), *Preventing violence: Research and evidence-based intervention strategies* (pp. 125–145). Washington, DC: American Psychological Association.

Farrell, A. D., Erwin, E. H., Bettencourt, A., Mays, S., Vulin-Reynolds, M., Sullivan, T. N., et al. (2008). Individual factors influencing effective non-violent behavior and fighting in peer situations: A qualitative study with urban African American adolescents. *Journal of Clinical Child and Adolescent Psychology, 37,* 397–411.

Farrell, A. D., Erwin, E. H., Mays, S., Bettencourt, A., Vulin-Reynolds, M., & Allison, K. W. (2008). Environmental influences on fighting versus nonviolent behavior in peer situations: A qualitative study with urban African American adolescents. Manuscript submitted for publication.

Farrell, A. D., Valois, R. F., Meyer, A. L., & Tidwell, R. P. (2003). Impact of the RIPP violence prevention program on rural middle school students. *Journal of Primary Prevention, 24,* 143–167.

Farrell, A. D., & Vulin-Reynolds, M. (2007). Violent behavior and the science of prevention. In D. Flannery, A. Vazsonyi, & I. Waldman (Eds.), *Cambridge handbook of violent behavior and aggression* (pp. 767–786). Cambridge: Cambridge University Press.

Finkenauer, C., Engels, R.C.M.E., & Baumeister, R. F. (2005). Parenting behaviour and adolescent behavioural and emotional problems: The role of self-control. *International Journal of Behavioral Development, 29,* 58–69.

Flannery, D. J., Vazsonyi, A. T., Liau, A. K., Guo, S., Powell, K. E., Atha, H., et al. (2003). Initial behavior outcomes for the PeaceBuilders universal school-based violence prevention program. *Developmental Psychology, 39,* 292–308.

Fontaine, R. G. (2006). Evaluative behavioral judgments and instrumental antisocial behaviors in children and adolescents. *Clinical Psychology Review, 26,* 956–967.

Fontaine, R. G., & Dodge, K. A. (2006). Real-time decision making and aggressive behavior in youth: A heuristic model of response evaluation and decision (RED). *Aggressive Behavior, 32,* 604–624.

Frey, K. S., Hirchstein, M. K., & Guzzo, B. A. (2000). Second Step: Preventing aggression by promoting social competence. *Journal of Emotional and Behavioral Disorders, 8,* 102–112.

Gauthier, Y. (2003). Infant mental health as we enter the third millennium: Can we prevent aggression? *Infant Mental Health Journal, 24*, 296–308.

Gomez, R., & McLaren, S. (2007). The inter-relations of mother and father attachment, self-esteem and aggression during late adolescence. *Aggressive Behavior, 33*, 160–169.

Gorman-Smith, D., Henry, D. B., & Tolan, P. H. (2004). Exposure to community violence and violence perpetration: The protective effects of family functioning. *Journal of Clinical Child and Adolescent Psychology, 33*, 439–449.

Gottfredson, M. R. (2007). Self-control and criminal violence. In D. Flannery, A. Vazsonyi, & I. Waldman (Eds.), *Cambridge handbook of violent behavior and aggression* (pp. 533–544). Cambridge: Cambridge University Press.

Guerra, N. G., Nucci, L., & Huesmann, L. R. (1994). Moral cognition and childhood aggression. In L. R. Huesmann (Ed.), *Current perspectives on aggressive behavior* (pp. 13–33). New York: Plenum.

Guerra, N. G., & Smith, E. P. (2005). *Preventing violence in a multi-cultural society.* Washington, DC: APA Books.

Hahn, R., Fuqua-Whitley, D., Wethington, H., Lowy, J., Crosby, A., Fullilove, M., et al. (2007). Effectiveness of universal school-based programs to prevent violent and aggressive behavior: A systematic review. *American Journal of Preventive Medicine, 33*, 114–129.

Hammond, W. R., & Yung, B. R. (1991). Preventing violence in at-risk African-American youth. *Journal of Health Care for the Poor and Underserved, 2*, 359–373.

Hanish, L. D., & Guerra, N. G. (2002). A longitudinal analysis of patterns of adjustment following peer victimization. *Development and Psychopathology, 14*, 69–89.

Hawkins, J. D., Catalano, R. F., Morrison, D. M., O'Donnell, J., Abbott, R., & Day, L. E. (1992). The Seattle Social Development Project: Effects of the first four years on protective factors and problem behaviors. In J. McCord & R. Tremblay (Eds.), *Preventing antisocial behavior: Interventions from birth through adolescence* (pp. 139–161). New York: Guilford Press.

Huesmann, L. R. (1998). The role of social information processing and cognitive schema in the acquisition and maintenance of habitual aggressive behavior. In R. G. Geen & E. Donnerstein (Eds.), *Human aggression: Theories, research, and implications for social policy* (pp. 73–109). Orlando, FL: Academic Press.

Huesmann, L. R., & Guerra, N. G. (1997). Social norms and children's aggressive behavior. *Journal of Personality and Social Psychology, 72*, 408–419.

Juvonen, J., & Graham, S. (2001). *Peer harassment in school: The plight of the vulnerable and victimized child.* New York: Guilford Press.

Kellam, S. G., Ling, X., Merisca, R., Brown, C. H., & Ialongo, N. (1998). The effect of the level of aggression in the first grade classroom on the course and malleability of aggressive behavior into middle school. *Development and Psychopathology, 10*, 165–185.

Kohlberg, L., & Kramer, R. (1969). Continuities and discontinuities in childhood and adult moral development. *Human Development, 12*, 3–120.

Laible, D. J., Carlo, G., & Raffaelli, M. (2000). The differential relations of parent and peer attachment to adolescent adjustment. *Journal of Youth and Adolescence, 29*, 45–59.

Lemerise, E. A., & Arsenio, W. F. (2000). An integrated model of emotion processes and cognition in social information processing. *Child Development, 71*, 107–118.

Lerner, R. M., & Castellino, D. R. (2002). Contemporary developmental theory and adolescence: Developmental systems and applied developmental science. *Journal of Adolescent Health, 31*, 122–135.

Losel, F., Bliesener, T., & Bender, D. (2007). Social information processing, experiences of aggression in social contexts, and aggressive behavior in adolescents. *Criminal Justice and Behavior, 34*, 330–347.

Ludwig, K. B., & Pittman, J. F. (1999). Adolescent prosocial values and self-efficacy in relation to delinquency, risky sexual behavior, and drug use. *Youth and Society, 30*, 461–482.

Malecki, C. K., & Demaray, M. K. (2004). The role of social support in the lives of bullies, victims, and bully-victims. In D. Espelage & S. Swearer (Eds.), *Bullying in American schools: A social-ecological perspective on prevention and intervention* (pp. 211–225). Mahwah, NJ: Erlbaum.

McMahon, S. D., & Washburn, J. J. (2003). Violence prevention: An evaluation of program effects with urban African American students. *Journal of Primary Prevention, 24*, 43–62.

Metropolitan Area Child Study Research Group. (2002). A cognitive-ecological approach to preventing aggression in urban settings: Initial outcomes for high-risk children. *Journal of Consulting and Clinical Psychology, 70*, 179–194.

Meyer, A. L., Farrell, A. D., Northup, W., Kung, E., & Plybon, L. (2000). *Promoting nonviolence in early adolescence: Responding in peaceful and positive ways*. New York: Kluwer.

Moffitt, T. (1993). Adolescent-limited versus life-course persistent antisocial behavior. *Psychological Review, 100*, 674–701.

Nelson, D. A., & Crick, N. R. (1999). Rose-colored glasses: Examining the social information-processing of prosocial young adolescents. *Journal of Early Adolescence, 19*, 17–38.

Orobio de Castro, B., Merk, W., Koops, W., Veerman, J. W., & Bosch, J. D. (2005). Emotions in social information processing and their relations with reactive and proactive aggression in referred aggressive boys. *Journal of Clinical Child and Adolescent Psychology, 34*, 105–116.

Pardini, D. A., Lochman, J. E., & Frick, P. J. (2003). Callous/unemotional traits and social-cognitive processes in adjudicated youths. *Journal of the American Academy of Child and Adolescent Psychiatry, 42*, 364–371.

Pepler, D. J., Madsen, K. C., Webster, C., & Levene, K. S. (2005). *The development and treatment of girlhood aggression*. Mahwah, NJ: Erlbaum.

Tolan, P. H., Gorman-Smith, D., & Henry, D. B. (2003). The developmental-ecology of urban males' youth violence. *Developmental Psychology, 39*, 274–291.

Tolan, P. H., & Guerra, N. (1994). *What works in reducing adolescent violence: An empirical review of the field*. Boulder, CO: Centers for the Study and Prevention of Violence, Institute for Behavioral Sciences.

Turiel, E. (1989). Domain-specific social judgments and domain ambiguities. *Merrill-Palmer Quarterly, 35*, 89–114.

van Ijzendoorn, M. H. (1997). Attachment, emergent morality, and aggression: Toward a developmental socioemotional model of antisocial behaviour. *International Journal of Behavioral Development, 21*, 703–727.

Wilson, S. J., & Lipsey, M. W. (2007). School-based interventions for aggressive and disruptive behavior: Update of a meta-analysis. *American Journal of Preventive Medicine, 33*(Suppl. 2), S130–S143.

TERRI N. SULLIVAN *is an assistant professor of psychology at Virginia Commonwealth University.*

ALBERT D. FARRELL *is a professor of psychology and the director of the Clark-Hill Institute for Positive Youth Development at Virginia Commonwealth University.*

AMIE F. BETTENCOURT *is a graduate student in psychology at Virginia Commonwealth University.*

SARAH W. HELMS *is a graduate student in psychology at Virginia Commonwealth University.*

Haegerich, T. M., & Tolan, P. H. (2008). Core competencies and the prevention of adolescent substance use. In N. G. Guerra & C. P. Bradshaw (Eds.), *Core competencies to prevent problem behaviors and promote positive youth development*. New Directions for Child and Adolescent Development, 122, 47–60.

Core Competencies and the Prevention of Adolescent Substance Use

Tamara M. Haegerich, Patrick H. Tolan

Abstract

Adolescence is a developmental period during which youth are at increased risk for using substances. An empirical focus on core competencies illustrates that youth are less likely to use substances when they have a positive future orientation, a belief in the ability to resist substances, emotional and behavioral control, sound decision-making ability, a belief that substance use is wrong, and a strong bond to prosocial peers and family. Such etiological research is beginning to provide a strong foundation for successful competence-building prevention programs. Focusing on the developmental-ecological context of adolescent substance use will expedite advances in prevention. © Wiley Periodicals, Inc.

The findings and conclusions in this chapter are those of the authors and do not necessarily represent the official position of the Centers for Disease Control and Prevention.

In March 2007, the U.S. surgeon general issued a call to action on adolescent substance use, citing the high prevalence and negative effects of drinking on development (U.S. Department of Health and Human Services, 2007). Although the prevalence of smoking and drinking has declined since the late 1980s and early 1990s and a majority of teens disapprove of substance use, the accessibility to and use of cigarettes and alcohol among adolescents remains high, and signs of increased use of some illicit drugs such as narcotics and sedatives are worrisome (Johnston, O'Malley, Bachman, & Schulenberg, 2007).

Adolescence is a time of transition when youth develop identity, seek autonomy, and forge peer relationships (Steinberg, 2005). It is also a time of heightened risk for using alcohol, tobacco, and illicit drugs. Although some consider experimentation with substances to be a normal part of adolescent development (Tolan & Morris, 2005), early and prolonged use of substances is likely to result in problem behaviors and negative health outcomes, including drug-related emergency room visits, motor vehicle accidents, homicide, suicide, weapon carrying, fighting, and less seatbelt use (Centers for Disease Control and Prevention, 2004; DuRant, Smith, Kreiter, & Krowchuk, 1999; Hingson & Kenkel, 2004; Mallonee & Calvin, 2006). Early use and substance use disorder in adolescence have been associated with internalizing problems, less education, greater unemployment, and less life satisfaction in adulthood (Rohde et al., 2007; Trim, Meehan, King, & Chassin, 2007). It is critical to understand and differentiate between substance use initiation and experimentation and substance use problems. National surveys and longitudinal studies are shedding light on these distinctions by asking adolescents about their lifetime, current, and habitual use of substances.

Findings from the 2005 national Youth Risk Behavior Survey (YRBS; Centers for Disease Control and Prevention, 2006) indicate that slightly more than half of participating high school youth had tried a cigarette, yet 23 percent of youth reported current use and 9 percent reported current habitual use (smoking at least twenty of the thirty days preceding the survey). Slightly less than 40 percent had tried marijuana, with 20 percent reporting current use. A much higher 74 percent had had at least one drink of alcohol in their lifetime, with 43 percent reporting current use and 26 percent reporting current episodic heavy drinking (consuming five or more drinks of alcohol within a couple of hours). Prevalence of lifetime illicit drug use, such as cocaine, inhalants, heroin, methamphetamine, or ecstasy, is substantially lower, with 2 to 12 percent of youth reporting use. The majority of youth indicated that initiation of cigarette, alcohol, and drug use occurred at thirteen years of age or older (Centers for Disease Control and Prevention, 2006). Boys have somewhat higher rates of smokeless tobacco and illicit drug use than girls, particularly steroid use. The rates of smoking, drinking, and illicit drug use are lower among African American students than non-Hispanic White students, with rates of use among Hispanic students more similar to, and sometimes greater than, that of White students (Centers for Disease Control and Prevention, 2006; Johnston et al., 2007).

In applying a developmental-ecological perspective to promote prevention (Tolan, Szapocznik, & Sambrano, 2007), we review theories of adolescent substance use and etiological research highlighting the core competencies framework proposed in this volume: a positive sense of self, self-control, decision-making skills, a moral system of belief, and prosocial connectedness. We discuss prevention strategies for substance use that promote these competencies and conclude with suggestions for future research.

Theoretical Perspectives on Adolescent Substance Use

Theories of adolescent substance use have progressed dramatically during the past twenty-five years. Petraitis, Flay, and Miller (1995) conducted perhaps one of the most comprehensive reviews of substance use theories, leading to the categorization of theories as cognitive-affective, social learning, conventional commitment and social attachment, and intrapersonal characteristics. As described by Petraitis et al. (1995), these theories posit that adolescents' decisions to use substances are driven by their attitudes toward substances, expectations about their ability to use and benefits from use, affective value placed on the expected benefits of use, and beliefs about resistance to peer pressure; the influence of the attitudes and behaviors of others; the strength of conventional bonds to societal institutions and other people; and adolescents' own individual characteristics. Many of these theories highlight the importance of social context. Youth who come from socially disorganized communities, believe they lack the opportunities to reach their aspirations, and are bonded to deviant peers are at increased risk for substance use and abuse. Finally, integrated theories highlighted by Petraitis et al. (1995), such as Jessor and Jessor's problem behavior theory (1977), emphasize that the clustering of problem behaviors results from interactions between individuals and their environments.

Since the Petraitis et al. (1995) review, integrated models have grown in popularity. An example is developmental psychopathology models that posit that individual factors such as temperaments, cognitions, and personalities and environmental factors such as peer, family, and community, both proximal and distal, mutually influence one another at multiple layers of the social ecology and over the course of development (Glantz & Leshner, 2000). The developmental psychopathology model is part of the larger set of developmental-ecological models, stemming from Bronfenbrenner's ecological systems theory (1979), that have been applied to other adolescent problem behaviors, such as youth violence (Tolan, Guerra, & Kendall, 1995; Tolan & Gorman-Smith, 2002).

Until the mid-1990s, theories focused primarily on identifying risk factors, such as peer and parent use, substance availability, and neighborhood disorganization, that increase the probability of youth initiating and using substances, rather than framing the problem within a youth development approach (Hawkins, Catalano, & Miller, 1992). Researchers later began to shift their focus to youths' assets (Kim, Crutchfield, Williams, & Hepler, 1998; Catalano, Berglund, Ryan, Lonczak, & Hawkins, 1999). Consistent with the overarching theme in this volume, current scholars acknowledge that focusing on both risk and protection is critical to understanding and preventing substance use (Pollard & Hawkins, 1999).

Our focus on adolescent core competencies reflects an integrated approach to understanding substance use, with an emphasis on individual strengths and assets and an assumption that adolescents' personal characteristics are influenced by variables that exist across different levels of the social ecology and at different points in development. Although adolescents have their own individual strengths, families, peers, schools, culture, and society are strong socializing agents that can influence adolescents' core competencies.

Linking the Core Competencies with Adolescent Substance Use

The literature examining the influence of core competencies on substance use largely has been disjointed and typically focused on a select number of intrapersonal characteristics alone or in combination with other factors. Some investigations have been theoretically driven, while others have taken a more generic risk-factor approach. Cross-sectional and short-term longitudinal approaches are common, and thus limit causal conclusions. More recent research has investigated interactions among risk, protection, and the environment, as well as mediating and moderating processes. As we detail, the limited rigorous research available suggests that several aspects of the core competencies are important for protecting youth from engaging in substance use. Understanding the influence of such youth assets is critical for making advances in the development of successful prevention strategies.

A Positive Sense of Self. Although empiricists know that substance use can affect future goal attainment such as employment (Rohde et al., 2007), adolescents must decide for themselves whether using substances will inhibit their ability to achieve their goals and become the persons they would like to become. Youth who have high aspirations for staying in school are less likely to drink (Oman et al., 2004). Strong family relationships are associated with adolescents' positive life orientation; these beliefs, in turn, are associated with bonding to conventional peers and less substance use (Kogan, Luo, Murry, & Brody, 2005). When young adolescents believe that substance use will interfere with their future aspirations and is incongruent with their preferred lifestyle, they are less likely to use in late adolescence (Henry, Swaim, & Slater, 2005; McNeal & Hansen, 1999). A positive future orientation is also associated with less serious alcohol use and less engagement in alcohol-related risk behaviors such as frequent drunkenness, hard drug use, and having sex while drinking (Robbins & Bryan, 2004).

To achieve goals and future aspirations, individuals must believe that they can control their own actions and environment (Bandura, 2001). If substance use interferes with an adolescent's future aspirations, he or she must have a sense of agency to refrain from use. Indeed, resistance efficacy—an adolescent's belief that he or she can refuse substances—is associated with less concurrent and subsequent smoking, drinking, and illicit drug use (Barkin, Smith, & DuRant, 2002; Carvajal et al., 2004; Epstein, Zhou, Bang, & Botvin, 2007; Scheier, Botvin, Diaz, & Griffin, 1999; Wills, Gibbons, Gerrard, & Brody, 2000).

There is little evidence to suggest that a global sense of self-esteem is a promotive factor. Researchers have found effects contrary to expectations. Scheier and colleagues (2000) found higher esteem to be associated with increasing substance use, whereas Ludden and Eccles (2007) found that it did not differentiate nonusers from initiators, users, or desisters. Self-esteem has also been included with other intrapersonal variables in multivariate models, making it difficult to draw conclusions about the potential promotive value (Brody & Ge, 2001; Fearnow-Kenney, Hansen, & McNeal, 2002).

Self-Control. The ability to regulate emotions and behaviors may ultimately predict whether substance use is initiated either directly or indirectly through other mediating variables. Adolescents who have good generalized self-control in everyday situations are less likely to experience negative life events, which can drive youth to associate with substance-using peers who can lead them to use substances (Wills et al., 2000).

Adolescents with a diminished ability to control their emotions and communicate are more likely to drink and smoke marijuana (Fishbein et al., 2006). For example, adolescents who are better able to manage their stress, anger, and sadness are more likely to do well in school, associate with peers who do not use substances, and experience more positive life events and, in turn, are less likely to smoke and drink. Adolescents who exhibit greater planfulness, problem-solving ability, cognitive effort, and self-reinforcement are also more likely to be academically competent, experience positive life events, and resist substances (Wills, Walker, Mendoza, & Ainette, 2006). Behavioral control has also been linked to reductions in more severe alcohol use, social problems associated with drinking, and symptomatic drinking (Brody & Ge, 2001).

Decision-Making Skills. Better decision-making skills early in adolescence are predictive of greater refusal assertiveness, frequent drinking, and frequent smoking later in development (Epstein, Griffin, & Botvin, 2000a, 2000b). Early-onset users tend to exhibit poorer decision-making skills than both nonusers and new users (Sobeck, Abbey, Agius, Clinton, & Harrison, 2000). When adolescents are more likely to perceive that drinking will result in social benefits, good decision-making abilities are particularly protective (Epstein et al., 2007). Some research suggests, however, that perceived decision-making skills are more predictive of anticipated use than of current use (Barkin et al., 2002).

A Moral System of Belief. The research suggests that youth view substance use as more of a personal choice to engage in risky behavior than an issue of moral judgment (Kuther & Higgins-D'Alessandro, 2000). Yet a stronger belief that substance use is morally wrong and a more general belief in the moral order (for example, that it is wrong to cheat and important to tell the truth) has been associated with less substance use (Abide, Richards, & Ramsay, 2001; Beyers, Toumbourou, Catalano, Arthur, & Hawkins, 2004). Moral beliefs also have been found to mediate the effects of bonding to prosocial individuals and activities on substance use (Catalano, Kosterman, Hawkins, Newcomb, & Abbott, 1996). Intolerance of deviance more generally has been linked with less problem drinking (Costa, Jessor, & Turbin, 1999).

Prosocial Connectedness. Catalano and colleagues (1996) were among the first to examine the importance of social connectedness in protecting youth from substance use with the introduction of the social development model. They theorized that families, schools, and other social groups and institutions serve as strong socializing agents. With consistent socialization and involvement over time, adolescents form bonds that deter them from violating the norms and values established by those groups and institutions. Tests of this model indicate that prosocial interaction skills predict prosocial socialization (opportunities, involvement, and rewards) and socialization predicts prosocial bonding to peers, family, schools, and neighborhoods. In turn, prosocial bonding predicts belief in the moral order (commitment to the values of the socialization agents), which then predicts less substance use (Catalano et al., 1996).

Other complementary research suggests that adolescents who are bonded to school are more likely to believe that substance use will interfere with their future aspirations and less likely to associate with substance-using peers; they also use less tobacco, alcohol, and marijuana (Henry et al., 2005; Shears, Edwards, & Stanley, 2006). School bonding has been found to mediate the effects of self-control on substance use (Wang, Matthew, Bellamy, & James, 2005).

Good family communication, family warmth, joint activities, and support predict less initiation and excessive use of alcohol and illicit drugs (Guo, Hill, Hawkins, Catalano, & Abbott, 2002; Kuntsche & Kuendig, 2006; Oman et al., 2004). These factors may be particularly protective for youth who have not already experienced high levels of social disintegration (Hüsler, Plancherel, & Werlen, 2005). Parental emotional support has been found to reduce substance use indirectly by promoting good behavioral and emotional control, which affects positive life orientation and events and bonding with conventional peers and institutions (schools). Such bonding reduces the likelihood of engaging in substance use (Kogan et al., 2005; Wang et al., 2005; Wills et al., 2000, 2006).

Researchers also have examined the effects of religiosity on adolescent substance use (Beyers et al., 2004; Kogan et al., 2005), with some suggesting that participation in religious services may be particularly protective for girls

(Oman et al., 2004) and may buffer the effects of neighborhood disorder on illicit drug use (Jang & Johnson, 2001). More studies are needed, however, to better understand how bonding to religious institutions may be protective. Such an understanding is particularly important given the role of religion in alcohol treatment programs, the importance of religion in some cultures, the social resources available through religious involvement, and the interest of the public health community in the relation between religious involvement and health more generally (Chatters, 2000).

Role of Core Competencies in Adolescent Substance Use Prevention

Preliminary efforts to prevent substance use among adolescents focused on direct instruction about the negative effects of substance use on health. These efforts were, however, largely ineffective (one example was Drug Abuse Resistance Education, DARE) (West & O'Neal, 2004). Over time, etiological research on adolescent competencies has provided a stronger foundation for evidence-based prevention programming. One of the largest collaborative efforts to integrate core competencies into a prevention model emanated from a multisite evaluation of preventive interventions that aim to enhance behavioral self-regulation, parental involvement, school bonding, and social competence among children and youth (Tarter, Sambrano, & Dunn, 2002). Two programs, Schools and Families Educating Children (SAFEChildren; Gorman-Smith et al., 2002) and Coping Power (Lochman & Wells, 2002), are particularly instructive.

The SAFEChildren program is a family-focused intervention, with an academic tutoring supplement, for first-grade children in their transition into elementary school. Guided by developmental-ecological theories, the intervention aims to improve family relationships, children's academic achievement and school bonding, family involvement in school, and ultimately children's self-control and social competence, which are believed to reduce substance use later in adolescence (Gorman-Smith et al., 2007). Initial impacts from a randomized trial suggest improvements in reading ability for children and stable school involvement for parents participating in the intervention, with additional improvements in aggression and hyperactivity for high-risk children (Tolan, Gorman-Smith, & Henry, 2004). The investigators predict that continued reductions in externalizing behavior problems, coupled with improvements in self-control, social competence, and achievement, will result in lower levels of substance use as the children reach adolescence.

The Coping Power program, a universal school-based parent and classroom program for fifth- and sixth-grade adolescents, with a targeted child and parent intervention for at-risk youth and their families, focuses on improving social bonds among youth, families, and schools. The universal program includes teacher in-service training and classroom parent meetings. The targeted intervention for high-risk youth and their families consists of one-on-one and group sessions with children, parent group sessions, and home visits. The program aims to improve social competence, self-regulation, decision making, school bonding, and parental involvement (Lochman, Wells, & Murray, 2007). A randomized trial documented improvements in social competence, self-regulation, and parenting for children and parents who received either the universal program or the targeted intervention, or both. Youth who received intervention used significantly less alcohol, tobacco, and marijuana in the prior month than youth who did not receive the intervention (Lochman & Wells, 2002).

Other competency-focused family and school-based programs have shown promise in reducing cigarette, alcohol, illicit, and polydrug use by delaying, reducing, or slowing the progression of use. Such programs include the Life Skills Training, Preparing for the Drug Free Years, and the Strengthening Families Program, which focus on building self-esteem, resistance efficacy, and family bonding and communication (Botvin et al., 2000; Kumpfer, Alvarado, Tait, & Whiteside, 2007; Mason, Kosterman, Hawkins, Haggerty, & Spoth, 2003; see Foxcroft, Ireland, Lister-Sharp, Lowe, & Breen, 2003, and Skara & Sussman, 2003, for meta-analytic findings and reviews).

Programs that foster core competencies are more effective than noninteractive, didactic instruction programs that focus on knowledge of the effects of substance use (Tobler et al., 2000) and can be particularly effective for high-risk youth (Gottfredson & Wilson, 2003). Although many intervention programs focus on core competencies and result in favorable outcomes, few researchers have systematically examined the mediating mechanisms purported to produce effects. When mediation models have been tested, youths' normative beliefs about the use of substances and resistance efficacy have emerged as potentially important mediators (Botvin, Griffin, Diaz, & Iffil-Williams, 2001; Donaldson, Graham, & Hansen, 1994; Komro et al., 2001; Orlando, Ellickson, McCaffrey, & Longshore, 2005).

Future Directions

Significant progress has been made in the past twenty-five years, yet a focus on the core competencies that protect youth and promote healthy development has been limited. We must continue to examine how core competencies promote adolescent development and protect against substance use and build on the increasing set of empirically tested and developmentally informed prevention approaches (Tolan et al., 2007).

Etiological research has been limited by theoretical emphasis on risk problems and failures rather than formulating how typical and normative healthy development occurs. Furthermore, when competencies are examined, the measurement techniques employed (for example, limited self-report survey questions that vary across studies) often are inadequate. With emerging evidence suggesting that core competencies can play a key role, it is important to more thoroughly examine those competencies with more sophisticated measurement strategies.

Mediating and moderating processes are yet to be uncovered that explain the interplay among competencies, culture, and contextual factors. It is unclear which competencies are critical in developing a youth's ability to bond to family and school and accept the conventional values that those institutions enforce. We must also better understand family and community factors that affect youths' competencies. Our understanding of how culture affects substance use is also incomplete given the narrow focus on racial and ethnic differences without situating them in a broader cultural context or empirically testing cultural theories (see De La Rosa, 2002). Examining interactive processes will advance the field's understanding of how culture and context affect development and substance use and inform prevention strategies.

Research examining when competencies may be maladaptive remains quite sparse. Youth violence research has highlighted ways in which peer competence such as popularity may increase the propensity for aggression (Guerra, Boxer, & Cook, 2006). Parallel work is indicated in the substance use field, particularly because adolescents' bonding with substance-using peers is such a strong predictor of substance use (Dishion, Capaldi, Spracklen, & Li, 1995).

Perhaps the areas most in need of careful integration are the developmental and epidemiological research perspectives that show that most adolescents (and adults) engage in some substance use (Tolan et al., 2007) and that most of those who engage in problematic use and overindulgence cease by early adulthood (Tolan & Morris, 2005). The cause of this desistance is unclear. Is it because of natural contingencies (negative reinforcement due to problems and physical impositions due to overuse)? Is it changing norms as one ages? Or is it the adoption of conventional adult roles that lead to this general tendency to decrease use with age? Related to this general developmental trend is the recovery of many high-risk youth. A substantial proportion of those who exhibit high risk during adolescence show satisfactory functioning by early adulthood (Tolan et al., 2007). Continued application of developmental-ecological theory to understand the etiology of adolescent substance use will lead to further improvements in the development and application of appropriate intervention strategies. In addition, longer-term and more intensive study of natural development and preventive effects on risk behaviors can illuminate key risk and protective factors and the variety of outcomes among those who use substances (Tolan & Gorman-Smith, 2002). These findings can further refine developmentally attuned prevention (Tolan et al., 2007).

Finally, our developmentally and ecologically informed understanding of the core competencies and the relations among competencies, other protective factors, and substance use behaviors is still quite basic, with limited empirical study. Few randomized prevention trials have demonstrated sizable effects on adolescent substance use. By recognizing the complex etiology of substance use and shifting prevention activities toward a consideration of the developmental-ecological context, we may expedite advances in defining the problem, identifying protective and promotive factors, and developing and testing prevention programs. These advances may more reliably and effectively guide future work to ensure widespread adoption of evidence-based prevention approaches.

References

Abide, M. M., Richards, H. C., & Ramsay, S. G. (2001). Moral reasoning and consistency of belief and behavior: Decisions about substance abuse. *Journal of Drug Education, 31,* 367–384.

Bandura, A. (2001). Social cognitive theory: An agentic perspective. *Annual Review of Psychology, 52,* 1–26.

Barkin, S., Smith, K. S., & DuRant, R. H. (2002). Social skills and attitudes associated with substance use behaviors among young adolescents. *Journal of Adolescent Health, 30,* 448–454.

Beyers, J. M., Toumbourou, J. W., Catalano, R. F., Arthur, M. W., & Hawkins, J. D. (2004). A cross-national comparison of risk and protective factors for adolescent substance use: The United States and Australia. *Journal of Adolescent Health, 35,* 3–16.

Botvin, G. J., Griffin, K. W., Diaz, T., & Iffil-Williams, M. (2001). Drug abuse prevention among minority adolescents: Posttest and one-year follow-up of a school-based preventive intervention. *Prevention Science, 2,* 1–13.

Botvin, G. J., Griffin, K. W., Diaz, T., Scheier, L. M., Williams, C., & Epstein, J. A. (2000). Preventing illicit drug use in adolescents: Long-term follow-up data from a randomized control trial of a school population. *Addictive Behaviors, 25,* 769–774.

Brody, G. H., & Ge, X. (2001). Linking parenting processes and self-regulation to psychological functioning and alcohol use during early adolescence. *Journal of Family Psychology, 115,* 82–94.

Bronfenbrenner, U. (1979). *The ecology of human development.* Cambridge, MA: Harvard University Press.

Carvajal, S. C., Hanson, C., Downing, R. A., Coyle, K. K., & Pederson, L. L. (2004). Theory-based determinants of youth smoking: A multiple influence approach. *Journal of Applied Social Psychology, 34,* 59–84.

Catalano, R. F., Berglund, M. L., Ryan, J.A.M., Lonczak, H. S., & Hawkins, J. D. (1999). *Positive youth development in the United States.* Washington, DC: U.S. Department of Health and Human Services.

Catalano, R. F., Kosterman, R., Hawkins, J. D., Newcomb, M. D., & Abbott, R. D. (1996). Modeling the etiology of adolescent substance use: A test of the social development model. *Journal of Drug Issues, 26,* 429–455.

Centers for Disease Control and Prevention. (2004). *National Center for Injury Prevention and Control Web-Based Injury Statistics Query and Reporting System (WISQARS), 1999–2004.* Retrieved April 6, 2008, from www.cdc.gov/ncipc/wisqars/default.htm.

Centers for Disease Control and Prevention. (2006). Youth risk behavior surveillance—United States, 2005. *Morbidity and Mortality Weekly Report, 55*(Suppl. 5), 1–112.

Chatters, L. M. (2000). Religion and public health: Public health research and practice. *Annual Review of Public Health, 21,* 335–367.

Costa, F. M., Jessor, R., & Turbin, M. S. (1999). Transition into adolescent problem drinking: The role of psychosocial risk and protective factors. *Journal of Studies on Alcohol, 60,* 480–490.

De La Rosa, M. (2002). Acculturation and Latino adolescents' substance use: A research agenda for the future. *Substance Use and Misuse, 37,* 429–456.

Dishion, T. J., Capaldi, D., Spracklen, K. M., & Li, F. (1995). Peer ecology of male adolescent drug use. *Development and Psychopathology, 7,* 803–824.

Donaldson, S. I., Graham, J. W., & Hansen, W. B. (1994). Testing the generalizability of intervening mechanism theories: Understanding the effects of adolescent drug use prevention interventions. *Journal of Behavioral Medicine, 17,* 195–216.

DuRant, R. H., Smith, J. A., Kreiter, S. R., & Krowchuk, D. P. (1999). The relationship between early age of onset of initial substance use and engaging in multiple health risk behaviors among young adolescents. *Archives of Pediatric Adolescent Medicine, 153,* 286–291.

Epstein, J. A., Griffin, K. W., & Botvin, G. J. (2000a). Role of general and specific competence skills in protecting inner-city adolescents from alcohol use. *Journal of Studies on Alcohol, 61,* 379–386.

Epstein, J. A., Griffin, K. W., & Botvin, G. J. (2000b). Competence skills help deter smoking among inner city adolescents. *Tobacco Control, 9,* 33–39.

Epstein, J. A., Zhou, X. K., Bang, H., & Botvin, G. J. (2007). Do competence skills moderate the impact of social influences to drink and perceived social benefits of drinking on alcohol use among inner-city adolescents? *Prevention Science, 8,* 65–73.

Fearnow-Kenney, M., Hansen, W. B., & McNeal, R. B. (2002). Comparison of psychosocial influences on substance use in adolescents: Implications for prevention programming. *Journal of Child and Adolescent Substance Abuse, 11,* 1–24.

Fishbein, D. H., Herman-Stahl, M., Eldreth, D., Paschall, J. J., Hyde, C., Hubal, R., et al. (2006). Mediators of the stress-substance-use relationship in urban male adolescents. *Prevention Science, 7,* 113–126.

Foxcroft, D. R., Ireland, D., Lister-Sharp, D. J., Lowe, G., & Breen, R. (2003). Longer-term primary prevention for alcohol misuse in young people: A systematic review. *Addiction, 98,* 397–411.

Glantz, M. D., & Leshner, A. I. (2000). Drug abuse and developmental psychopathology. *Development and Psychopathology, 12,* 795–814.

Gorman-Smith, D., Tolan, P., Henry, D. B., Leventhal, A., Schoeny, M., Lutovsky, K., et al. (2002). Predictors of participation in a family-focused preventive intervention for substance use. *Psychology of Addictive Behaviors, 16,* S55-S64.

Gorman-Smith, D., Tolan, P., Henry, D. B., Quintana, E., Lutovsky, K., & Leventhal, A. (2007). Schools and families educating children: A preventive intervention for early elementary school children. In P. Tolan, J. Szapocznik, & S. Sambrano (Eds.), *Preventing youth substance abuse* (pp. 113–135). Washington, DC: American Psychological Association.

Gottfredson, D. C., & Wilson, D. B. (2003). Characteristics of effective school-based substance abuse prevention. *Prevention Science, 4,* 27–38.

Guerra, N., Boxer, P., & Cook, C. R. (2006). What works (and what does not) in youth violence prevention: Rethinking the questions and finding new answers. In C. Hudley & R. N. Parker (Eds.), *Pitfalls and pratfalls: Null and negative findings in evaluating interventions* (pp. 59–71). New Directions for Evaluation, no. 11. San Francisco: Jossey-Bass.

Guo, J., Hill, K. G., Hawkins, D., Catalano, R. F., & Abbott, R. D. (2002). A developmental analysis of sociodemographic, family, and peer effects on adolescent illicit drug initiation. *Journal of the American Academy of Child and Adolescent Psychiatry, 41,* 838–845.

Hawkins, J. D., Catalano, R. F., & Miller, J. Y. (1992). Risk and protective factors for alcohol and other drug problems in adolescence and early adulthood: Implications for substance abuse prevention. *Psychological Bulletin, 112,* 64–105.

Henry, K. L., Swaim, R. C., & Slater, M. D. (2005). Intraindividual variability of school bonding and adolescents' beliefs about the effect of substance use on future aspirations. *Prevention Science, 6,* 101–112.

Hingson, R., & Kenkel, D. (2004). Social health and economic consequences of underage drinking. In R. J. Bonnie & M. E. O'Connell (Eds.), *Reducing underage drinking: A collective responsibility* (pp. 351–382). Washington, DC: National Academies Press.

Hüsler, G., Plancherel, B., & Werlen, E. (2005). Psychosocial predictors of cannabis use in adolescents at risk. *Prevention Science, 6,* 237–244.

Jang, S. J., & Johnson, B. R. (2001). Neighborhood disorder, individual religiosity, and adolescent use of illicit drugs: A test of multilevel hypotheses. *Criminology, 39,* 109–144.

Jessor, R., & Jessor, S. L. (1977). *Problem behavior and psychosocial development.* Orlando, FL: Academic Press.

Johnston, L. D., O'Malley, P. M., Bachman, J. G., & Schulenberg, J. E. (2007). *Monitoring the future national results on adolescent drug use: Overview of key findings, 2006.* Bethesda, MD: National Institute on Drug Abuse.

Kim, S., Crutchfield, C., Williams, C., & Hepler, N. (1998). Toward a new paradigm in substance abuse and other problem behavior prevention for youth: Youth development and empowerment approach. *Journal of Drug Education, 28,* 1–17.

Kogan, S. M., Luo, Z., Murry, V. M., & Brody, G. H. (2005). Risk and protective factors for substance use among African American high school dropouts. *Psychology of Addictive Behaviors, 19,* 382–391.

Komro, K. A., Perry, C. L., Williams, C. L., Stigler, M. H., Farbakhsh, K., & Veblen-Mortenson, S. (2001). How did Project Northland reduce alcohol use among young adolescents? Analysis of mediating variables. *Health Education Research, 16,* 59–70.

Kumpfer, K. L., Alvarado, R., Tait, C., & Whiteside, H. O. (2007). The Strengthening Families Program: An evidence-based multicultural family skills training program. In P. Tolan, J. Szapocznik, & S. Sambrano (Eds.), *Preventing youth substance abuse* (pp. 159–181). Washington, DC: American Psychological Association.

Kuntsche, E. N., & Kuendig, H. (2006). What is worse? A hierarchy of family-related risk factors predicting alcohol use in adolescence. *Substance Use and Misuse, 41,* 71–86.

Kuther, T. L., & Higgins-D'Alessandro, A. (2000). Bridging the gap between moral reasoning and adolescent engagement in risky behavior. *Journal of Adolescence, 23,* 409–422.

Lochman, J. E., & Wells, K. C. (2002). The Coping Power Program at the middle-school transition: Universal and indicated prevention effects. *Psychology of Addictive Behaviors, 16,* S40–S54.

Lochman, L. E., Wells, K. C., & Murray, M. (2007). The Coping Power Program: Preventive intervention at the middle school transition. In P. Tolan, J. Szapocznik, & S. Sambrano (Eds.), *Preventing youth substance abuse* (pp. 185–210). Washington, DC: American Psychological Association.

Ludden, A. B., & Eccles, J. S. (2007). Psychosocial, motivational, and contextual profiles of youth reporting different patterns of substance use during adolescence. *Journal of Research on Adolescence, 17,* 51–88.

Mallonee, E., & Calvin, S. (2006). Emergency department visits involving underage drinking. *New DAWN Report, 1,* 1–4.

Mason, W. A., Kosterman, R., Hawkins, J. D., Haggerty, K. P., & Spoth, R. L. (2003). Reducing adolescents' growth in substance use and delinquency: Randomized trial effects of a parent-training prevention intervention. *Prevention Science, 4,* 203–212.

McNeal, R. B., & Hansen, W. B. (1999). Developmental patterns associated with the onset of drug use: Changes in postulated mediators during adolescence. *Journal of Drug Issues, 29,* 381–400.

Oman, R. F., Vesely, S., Aspy, C. B., McLeroy, K. R., Rodine, S., & Marshall, L. (2004). The potential protective effect of youth assets on adolescent alcohol and drug use. *American Journal of Public Health, 94,* 1425–1430.

Orlando, M., Ellickson, P. L., McCaffrey, D. F., & Longshore, D. (2005). Mediation analysis of a school-based drug prevention program: Effects of Project Alert. *Prevention Science, 6,* 35–46.

Petraitis, J., Flay, B. R., & Miller, T. Q. (1995). Reviewing theories of adolescent substance use: Organizing pieces of the puzzle. *Psychological Bulletin, 117,* 67–86.

Pollard, J. A., & Hawkins, J. D. (1999). Risk and protection: Are both necessary to understand diverse behavioral outcomes in adolescence? *Social Work Research, 23,* 145–158.

Robbins, R. N., & Bryan, A. (2004). Relationships between future orientation, impulsive sensation seeking, and risk behavior among adjudicated adolescents. *Journal of Adolescent Research, 19,* 428–445.

Rohde, P., Lewinsohn, P. M., Seeley, J. R., Klein, D. N., Andrews, J. A., & Small, J. W. (2007). Psychological functioning of adults who experienced substance use disorders as adolescents. *Psychology of Addictive Behaviors, 21,* 155–164.

Scheier, L. M., Botvin, G. J., Diaz, T., & Griffin, K. W. (1999). Social skills, competence, and drug refusal efficacy as predictors of adolescent alcohol use. *Journal of Drug Education, 29,* 251–278.

Scheier, L. M., Botvin, G. J., Griffin, K. W., & Diaz, T. (2000). Dynamic growth models of self-esteem and adolescent alcohol use. *Journal of Early Adolescence, 20,* 178–209.

Shears, J., Edwards, R. W., & Stanley, L. R. (2006). School bonding and substance use in rural communities. *Social Work Research, 30,* 6–18.

Skara, S., & Sussman, S. (2003). A review of 25 long-term adolescent tobacco and other drug use prevention program evaluations. *Preventive Medicine, 37,* 451–474.

Sobeck, J., Abbey, A., Agius, E., Clinton, M., & Harrison, K. (2000). Predicting early adolescent substance use: Do risk factors differ depending on age of onset? *Journal of Substance Abuse, 11,* 89–102.

Steinberg, L. (2005). *Adolescence.* New York: McGraw-Hill.

Tarter, R. E., Sambrano, S., & Dunn, M. (2002). Predictor variables by developmental stages: A Center for Substance Abuse Prevention multisite study. *Psychology of Addictive Behaviors, 16,* S3–S10.

Tobler, N. S., Roona, M. R., Ochshorn, P, Marshall, D. G., Streke, A. V. & Stackpole, K. M. (2000). School-based adolescent drug prevention programs: 1998 meta-analysis. *Journal of Primary Prevention, 20,* 275–336.

Tolan, P. H., & Gorman-Smith, D. (2002). What violence prevention research can tell us about developmental psychopathology. *Development and Psychopathology, 14,* 713–729.

Tolan, P., Gorman-Smith, D., & Henry, D. (2004). Supporting families in a high-risk setting: Proximal effects of the SAFEChildren preventive intervention. *Journal of Consulting and Clinical Psychology, 72,* 855–869.

Tolan, P. H., Guerra, N. G., & Kendall, P. C. (1995). A developmental-ecological perspective on antisocial behavior in children and adolescents: Toward a unified risk and intervention framework. *Journal of Consulting and Clinical Psychology, 63,* 579–584.

Tolan, P., & Morris, K. (2005). The inner-city of the United States and risk for substance use among youth. In I. Obot & S. Saxena (Eds.), *Substance use among young people in urban environments* (pp. 77–102). Geneva: World Health Organization.

Tolan, P. H., Szapocznik, J., & Sambrano, S. (2007). Opportunities for development prevention of substance abuse. In P. Tolan, J. Szapocznik, & S. Sombrano (Eds.), *Preventing youth substance abuse: Science-based programs for children and adolescents* (pp. 241–252). Washington, DC: American Psychological Association.

Trim, R. S., Meehan, B. T., King, K. M., & Chassin, L. (2007). The relation between adolescent substance use and young adult internalizing symptoms: Findings from a high-risk longitudinal sample. *Psychology of Addictive Behaviors, 21,* 97–107.

U.S. Department of Health and Human Services. (2007). *The surgeon general's call to action to prevent and reduce underage drinking.* Rockville, MD: Author.

Wang, M. Q., Matthew, R. F., Bellamy, N., & James, S. (2005). A structural model of the substance use pathways among minority youth. *American Journal of Health Behavior, 29,* 531–541.

West, S. L., & O'Neal, K. K. (2004). Project D.A.R.E. outcome effectiveness revisited. *American Journal of Public Health, 94,* 1027–1029.

Wills, T. A., Gibbons, F. X., Gerrard, M., & Brody, G. H. (2000). Protection and vulnerability processes relevant for early onset of substance use: A test among African American children. *Health Psychology, 19,* 253–263.

Wills, T. A., Walker, C., Mendoza, D., & Ainette, M. G. (2006). Behavioral and emotional self-control: Relations to substance use in samples of middle and high school students. *Psychology of Addictive Behaviors, 20*, 265–278.

TAMARA M. HAEGERICH *is the special assistant to the associate director of science at the Division of Violence Prevention, National Center for Injury Prevention and Control, Centers for Disease Control and Prevention.*

PATRICK H. TOLAN *is the director of the Institute for Juvenile Research and professor in the Department of Psychiatry at the University of Illinois at Chicago.*

Charles, V. E., & Blum, R. W. (2008). Core competencies and the prevention of high-risk sexual behavior. In N. G. Guerra & C. P. Bradshaw (Eds.), *Core competencies to prevent problem behaviors and promote positive youth development.* New Directions for Child and Adolescent Development, 122, 61–74.

Core Competencies and the Prevention of High-Risk Sexual Behavior

Vignetta Eugenia Charles, Robert Wm. Blum

Abstract

Adolescent sexual risk-taking behavior has numerous individual, family, community, and societal consequences. In an effort to contribute to the research and propose new directions, this chapter applies the core competencies framework to the prevention of high-risk sexual behavior. It describes the magnitude of the problem, summarizes explanatory theories of high-risk sexual behavior, and highlights the association between high-risk sexual behaviors and the five core competencies. We conclude the chapter by providing an overview of selected evidence-based prevention strategies and identifying future directions for research and intervention. © Wiley Periodicals, Inc.

Adolescents have high rates of sexual risk taking, defined as an early age at sexual debut, having multiple sexual partners, and engaging in unprotected sex that puts them at risk for unplanned pregnancy and sexually transmitted infections (STIs) and the human immunodeficiency virus (HIV). Every year in the United States, approximately 750,000 adolescents aged fifteen to nineteen become pregnant. The vast majority (82 percent) of all adolescent pregnancies are unplanned, and more than one-quarter end in abortion (Guttmacher Institute, 2007). Overall, seventy-five pregnancies occur every year per one thousand women aged fifteen to nineteen; this rate has declined 36 percent since its peak in 1990 (Guttmacher Institute, 2007). Approximately 14 percent of the decline in teen pregnancy between 1995 and 2002 was due to teens' delaying sex or having sex less often, and 86 percent was due to an increase in sexually experienced teens' contraceptive use (Santelli, Lindberg, Finer, & Singh, 2007). Of the 18.9 million new cases of STIs each year, 9.1 million (48 percent) occur among fifteen to twenty-four year olds (Weinstock, Berman, & Cates, 2004).

There are significant racial and ethnic differences in youth sexual risk taking in the United States. Black women have the highest teen pregnancy rate (134 per 1,000 women aged fifteen to nineteen), followed by Hispanics (131 per 1,000) and non-Hispanic Whites (48 per 1,000) (Guttmacher Institute, 2007). Asian American adolescents report lower involvement with sexual activity than all other racial/ethnic peer groups. However, once they are initiated, Asian American adolescents have sexual behavior patterns comparable to other adolescent groups (Tosh & Simmons, 2007). Individual social and biological factors, such as age of menarche, as well as contextual factors, likely account for several of these racial and ethnic differences (Blum et al., 2000; Harlan, Harlan, & Grillo, 1980)

The research largely has framed all sexual behavior as problematic. Furthermore, most of the research has focused on individual risk factors that predispose young people to high-risk sexual behavior and have rarely explored the multisystem and transactional dynamics within and between individual factors and various contexts that contribute to adolescent sexual behavior. This chapter aims to fill these research gaps by applying the core competencies framework (a positive sense of self, self-control, decision-making skills, a moral system of belief, and prosocial connectedness) outlined in Chapter One of this volume.

We first summarize the leading theories related to risky sexual behavior in adolescence, apply the core competencies framework to the study of sexual risk behavior, and conclude with a discussion of research-based prevention models, policies, and promising areas for future research. Although research typically has focused on either individual or contextual risk factors, we also try to integrate and suggest linkages across multiple levels of an individual's developmental ecology. For example, we explore how contextual factors have an impact on the unfolding of individual characteristics, with a specific focus on the five core competencies.

Theoretical Perspectives on High-Risk Sexual Behavior

The literature on sexual risk taking is informed by multiple explanatory theories focused on various levels of the ecology of a youth's experience: individual, family, and schools, for example. Two theoretical frameworks focused on the individual level, the theory of reasoned action (Ajzen & Fishbein, 1980; Fishbein & Middlestadt, 1989) and its extension, the theory of planned behavior (Ajzen, 1991), are widely cited in research on HIV risk-related behaviors and condom use (Albarracin, Johnson, Fishbein, & Muellerleile, 2001; Villarruel, Jemmott, Jemmott, & Ronis, 2004). These theoretical models posit that specific behavioral intentions are the direct determinants of behaviors. Intentions are determined through the internal psychological process of integrating behavioral beliefs about the consequences of the behavior (attitudes), normative beliefs referring to the perceived social pressure to perform or not perform a behavior (subjective norms), and control beliefs about how difficult or easy it would be to perform the behavior (perceived behavioral control) (Jemmott et al., 2007). Intentions, subjective norms, and control beliefs closely mirror the competencies of decision making, a moral system of belief, and a positive sense of self (agency) described in Chapter One.

In contrast to individually based risk models, population-based approaches typically focus on contextual factors that influence sexual risk taking. Understanding contextual factors that influence the behaviors can improve treatment and prevention strategies and elucidate the extent to which individual factors play a role. Bronfenbrenner's (1989) ecological systems theory offers a multisystem approach to thinking about youth sexual risk-taking behavior. These systems include the microsystem (age, race, self-esteem, and religiosity), mesosystem (parent, peer, and school connectedness, romantic relationships), exosystem (government institutions), and macrosystem (sexual images in the media, abortion policies, cultural norms related to adolescent sexual activity). A multisystem perspective on youth sexual risk taking is increasingly common (Kotchick, Shaffer, Forehand, & Miller, 2001). Ecological factors in the youth's immediate social environment tend to have the strongest effect on adolescents' sexual behavior (Kirby, 2002). However, these approaches typically have not specified how contextual factors in these multiple systems translate into individual characteristics that influence behavior. The core competency approach framework is a potentially instructive approach for elucidating these connections.

Linking the Core Competencies with Sexual Risk-Taking Behavior

A Positive Sense of Self. A positive sense of self can prevent sexual risk taking and potentially mitigate its impact on development and adjustment. This can include multiple and interrelated constructs, such as self-efficacy, self-esteem, and self-concept. For example, drawing on Bandura's self-efficacy theory (1977), Reitman et al. (1996) found that adolescents who believed they could effectively take action to prevent or avoid HIV exposure had fewer sexual partners and reported more condom use than their peers who had lower self-efficacy. Similarly, general and AIDS-specific self-efficacy has also been found to relate to increased condom use among high-risk female minority youth (Overby & Kegeles, 1994). Although these studies focus more specifically on HIV and AIDS, it is likely that self-efficacy plays a similar role in preventing other risky sexual behaviors.

Self-esteem has often been examined in relationship to risky sexual behavior, particularly among adolescent females (Gardner, Frank, & Amankwaa, 1998). Studies have found a significant association between high self-esteem and safer sexual behavior, such as consistent condom use, during late adolescence (Gardner et al., 1998; McNair, Carter, & Williams, 1998; Miller, Forehand, & Kotchick, 2000). Several studies have shown that lower self-esteem may be associated with sexual risk taking among adolescent girls (Kowaleski-Jones & Mott, 1998). Furthermore, Ethier et al. (2006) found that adolescents who had lower self-esteem reported initiating sex earlier and having had risky partners.

The research linking high self-esteem with reduced sexual risk-taking behavior is far from definitive. Specifically, the empirical evidence suggests that using a unidimensional construct of self-esteem does not translate across all adolescents. Capturing the influence of contextual factors, such as racial/ethnic identity or relationships with sexual partners, on self-esteem may be more explanatory than focusing on the individual-level construct of self-esteem alone. Using a multidimensional construct to measure self-concept in a sample of African American girls, Salazar et al. (2004) found that self-concept was associated with refusal to have unprotected sex, as mediated by partner communication about sex. Because self-concept may encompass diverse but related constructs, such as self-esteem, ethnic identity, and body image, it may be instructive to use a multiconstruct approach when studying the adolescent sexual risk-taking behavior. Taken together, the research suggests that the core self-evaluation traits of positive self-esteem, self-efficacy, and multidimensional self-concept are critical for avoiding high-risk sexual behavior in adolescence.

Self-Control. The ability of an adolescent to self-regulate emotions has been linked to sexual risk-taking behaviors across multiple dimensions, including self-restraint and impulse control. Risky sexual behavior has been associated with poor self-regulation and low self-restraint in both early and late adolescence (Crockett, Raffaelli, & Shen, 2006; Raffaelli & Crockett, 2003). Similarly, Feldman and Brown (1993) found that male self-restraint, a dimension akin to emotional regulation and impulse control, at ages ten to eleven was inversely associated with the number of sexual partners four years later. Similarly, Jemmott, Jemmott, and Villarruel (2002) conducted a study of Latino college students and found that impulse control was a strong and positive predictor of condom use intentions and use at last intercourse.

Decision-Making Skills. Decision making in relation to sexual activity and contraceptive behavior involves numerous critical steps, including having the relevant information, weighing the alternatives, and committing to the decision. This process requires problem-solving abilities and is complicated by the fact that many youth are making decisions in sometimes stressful and volatile sexual situations.

Social problem solving emphasizes the connection between decision making and the development of social relationship skills. Significant associations between social problem solving and increased adolescent risk behaviors have been reported in the literature on multiple problem behaviors, including high-risk sexual behavior (Hollen & Hobbie, 1993). For example, Knauth, Skowron, and Escobar (2006) found that higher levels of social problem solving were related to fewer high-risk sexual behaviors. Conversely, Commendador (2007) examined decision making in relation to sexual activity and contraceptive behavior and found that maladaptive decision making was associated with decreased contraceptive use in sexually active adolescent females.

Related research by Luker (1977) suggests that the decision not to contracept is the result of a rational process of "cost accounting." Therefore, a deliberate decision not to contracept may occur if the perceived advantages of pregnancy outweigh the advantages of contracepting. The Luker model specifies that contraceptive decisions might be a rational assignment of advantages and disadvantages to contraceptive use and pregnancy. Philiber and Namerow (1990) found empirical support for this model among urban teens, which suggests that if adolescents do not think that their future is worth investing in, they are less likely to decide to contracept.

Contextual factors, such as poverty and values about early childbearing, also are important in decision making about sex. The opportunity costs of early parenthood may be minimal in a context where social and economic advancement opportunities are limited (Furstenberg, 1987). Indeed, some posit that for those who are poor and are not on an academic trajectory, the opportunity costs may be greater for delaying pregnancy than for early childbearing (Geronimus, 2003).

Decision-making skills are also linked to the other core competencies. Those who have a sense of self-esteem in their decision-making ability, that is, decisional self-esteem, are more likely to engage in vigilant decision making. Conversely, those who have low self-esteem experience more stress and are likely to engage in panicky or complacent decision making (Mann, Harmoni, & Power, 1989).

A Moral System of Belief. Adolescents' moral system of belief can be informed by their capacity for empathy and religiosity and has been linked to youth sexual risk-taking behavior. Although this topic is not widely researched, one relevant study found that White males with more empathetic relationships (measured by the youth's perception of their caring and ability to relate to friends and maintain those friendships) were significantly less likely to be involved in risky behavior. In addition, youth who reported not possessing this competency were significantly more likely to engage in risky sexual behaviors (Evans et al., 2004). Another study of college-age women found that the capacity for empathy was a significant predictor of birth control use (Hart & Hilton, 1988).

Although the specific factors influencing adolescents' empathic and moral beliefs related to sexual risk are not well understood, they could be informed by membership in a faith community. A positive connection between religiosity and prosocial behavior has been well established in the literature. For example, Sinha, Cnaan, and Gelles (2007) found that attendance in worship services and participation in a religious youth group were negatively correlated with sexual activity, whereas perception of the importance of religion was positively correlated with sexual activity. For Latino college students, religiosity has been positively associated with consistent condom use (Jemmott et al., 2002). Similarly, a study by McCree, Wingood, DiClemente, Davies, and Harrington (2003) found that adolescent females who had higher religiosity scores were significantly more likely to have higher self-efficacy in communicating with new, as well as steady, male partners about STDs, HIV, and pregnancy prevention and in refusing an unsafe sexual encounter. These adolescents were also more likely to possess more positive attitudes toward condom use, to have initiated sex at a later age, and to have used a condom in the past six months. Taken together, the research suggests that a moral system of belief, and more specifically religious engagement and religiosity, may be an important aspect of a moral system of belief in relation to the prevention of risky sexual behavior.

Prosocial Connectedness. Prosocial connectedness has been inversely associated with high-risk sexual behavior. The more connected youth are to parents, peers, romantic partners, schools, neighborhoods, and communities, the less likely they are to engage in risky sexual behaviors. Several studies have shown that parents exert significant influence on the sexual risk-related beliefs, attitudes, and behaviors of adolescents (Hutchinson, Jemmott, Jemmott, Braverman, & Fong, 2003; Hutchinson & Wood, 2007). Some of the critical parenting processes that are influential on the sexual risk process include parental monitoring (Aronowitz, Rennells, & Todd, 2006; DiClemente et al., 2001) and parental values about teen sex (Jaccard, Dittus, & Gordon, 1998). Parental monitoring and supervision have consistently been associated with reductions in STI and HIV risk for adolescents (DiClemente, Crosby, & Wingood, 2002; Yang, Stanton, Li, Cottrel, Galbraith, & Kaljee, 2007).

Adolescents who report higher levels of connectedness with parents also have lower rates of unprotected sexual intercourse (Hutchinson et al., 2003), engage in sexual intercourse with fewer partners (Crosby et al., 2001), and make safer sexual decisions overall (Perrino, Gonzalez-Soldevilla, Pantin, & Szapocznik, 2000; Resnick et al., 1997). Although some researchers have not found such an association (Newcomer & Udry, 1985), parent-teen sexual risk communication has been shown to influence adolescent sexual risk beliefs and behaviors. For example, adolescents whose parents openly discuss sexual matters with them are more likely to delay first sexual intercourse, have fewer sexual intercourse partners, and engage in responsible contraceptive behavior (Hutchinson et al., 2003; Murry, 1996).

Peers also serve as a source of connectedness that can be either protective or risky. Supportive friendships have been associated with fewer sexual partners (Henrich, Brookmeyer, Shrier, & Shahar, 2006). Yet other studies have found that affiliation with socially deviant peers is linked to a greater likelihood of sexual behavior (Rodgers, Rodgers, & Rowe, 1990; Whitbeck, Whitbeck, Conger, Simons, & Kao, 1993).

The study of adolescent romantic relationships is a burgeoning field that is informative in understanding youth connectedness and its relationship to sexual risk taking. Adolescents report preoccupation with romantic feelings and relationships, and they place considerable emphasis on the significance of these relationships in their lives (O'Sullivan & Brooks-Gunn, 2005). Surprisingly little is known about how social, sexual, and romantic events are intertwined or coordinated over the course of adolescents' relationships. Having a romantic relationship and the quality of that relationship are associated positively with romantic self-concept and, in turn, with feelings of self-worth (Connolly, Connolly, & Konarski, 1994; Harter & Harter, 1999; Kuttler, Kuttler, La Greca, & Prinstein, 1999). Longitudinal evidence indicates that by late adolescence, self-perceived competence in romantic relationships emerges as a reliable component of general competence (Masten et al., 1995) and can lead to less risky sexual behavior.

School connectedness can also have an impact on youth sexual risk-taking behavior. Research by Resnick et al. (1997) indicated that youth who felt connected to school were less likely to initiate early sexual intercourse and were more likely to use contraceptives when they did have sex. Furthermore, youth who are academically engaged, as indicated by their academic performance, are less likely to engage in risky sexual behavior (Luster & Small, 1994; Scaramella, Conger, Simons, & Whitbeck, 1998).

An additional contextual connection is one to the neighborhood. For many youth, connection to the neighborhood or community may be more salient than to that of the school. A growing body of literature shows that neighborhood conditions influence adolescent sexual risk-taking behavior (Brewster, 1994; Ku, Sonenstein, & Pleck, 1993; Wickrama, Merten, & Elder, 2005). For example, the risk of teen pregnancy appears to increase in a linear fashion, such that as the number of wage earners in a neighborhood declines to a level that can be considered a "tipping point," after which the risk for teen pregnancy doubles (Crane, 1991).

Role of Core Competencies in the Prevention of High-Risk Sexual Behavior

In order to tackle complex issues such as high-risk sexual behaviors, prevention programs and policies must be multicomponent and address the individual and contextual influences on youth high-risk sexual behavior. Prevention programming for the most part has focused primarily on formal sex education programs, parent-child communication, and peer interventions. Some programs emphasize the sexual antecedents of sexual risk taking, such as the sexual beliefs, attitudes, norms, and self-efficacy related to sexual behaviors, closely linked to the core competencies framework but with a specific focus on sexual content in different settings and formats (group sessions versus one-on-one). In contrast, service-learning programs address nonsexual antecedents, such as connections to adults or belief in the future, but without specific reference to sexuality. Yet research by Kirby (2002) suggests that addressing both sexual and nonsexual antecedents of sexual risk is critical to effective prevention. This can be accomplished through more focused attention to core competencies and how they facilitate effective responding in relation to sexuality.

There is evidence that service-learning, which integrates meaningful community service and involvement with sexual health instruction, may be an effective HIV and pregnancy-preventive intervention strategy. Service-learning is linked to the core competencies in multiple ways. It can foster a sense of connectedness to adults and communities and increase protective attitudes and skills through positive self-identity, self-efficacy, and empathy. A randomized trial by O'Donnell and colleagues indicated that at both the six-month (O'Donnell et al., 1999) and two-year (O'Donnell et al., 2002) follow-up, community youth service participants were more likely than controls to report that they were sexually abstinent or, if sexually active, that they always used protection. This suggests that in both the short and long terms, service-learning interventions have the potential to reduce sexual risk taking among urban adolescents.

Another promising program that focuses on prosocial connectedness is the Strong African-American Families (SAAF) program. SAAF offers a combination of racial socialization and parenting practices designed to reduce adolescent sexual risk behavior. The link to the core competencies is clear: fostering a positive sense of self through parental values transmission. In addition, the program explicitly incorporates the influence of race as an important contextual factor with an impact on sexual behavior. In a quasi-experimental study, parents who participated in SAAF reported increased adaptive universal and racially specific parenting as compared with controls. Changes in these parenting behaviors were associated indirectly with sexual risk behavior through adolescent self-pride, peer orientation, and sexual intent (Murry, Berkel, Brody, Gerrard, & Gibbons, 2007).

Local, state, and federal policies about sexuality education also have a dramatic impact on the type of prevention programs designed to reduce sexual risk taking that are available to youth. As mentioned earlier, decision making about sexual behavior is a complex process. Arming teens with comprehensive sexuality information, which teaches about both abstinence and contraception, aids in their sexual decision making. Comprehensive sexuality education focused on improving decision-making skills, relationships, and communication may facilitate more competent decision making.

In spite of the evidence base supporting comprehensive sexuality education, no federal program is dedicated to supporting these programs. Comprehensive sex education programs can help delay the onset of sexual activity among teens, reduce their number of sexual partners, and increase contraceptive use when they become sexually active (Kirby, 2001). In contrast, research suggests that abstinence-only strategies may actually deter contraceptive use among sexually active teens, thereby increasing their risk of unintended pregnancy and STIs (Trenholm et al., 2007). In spite of the evidence, by 2002 it was estimated that one-third of teens had not received any formal instruction about contraception (Guttmacher Institute, 2006). In sum, programs and policies aiming to prevent high-risk sexual behavior should be evidence based, foster the development of the core competencies, and address key contextual influences.

Future Directions

The research on youth sexual risk taking is rich and diverse, and there are new areas to explore. To date, most of the literature has focused on individual-level risk factors and their relationships to specific negative outcomes. Without a clear exploration of the mechanisms by which both risk and protective factors function and the contexts in which youth live, it is unlikely that the research will provide a clear understanding of adolescent sexual risk behavior.

Much of the literature focuses on individual competencies and their unique contribution as predictors of the outcome of sexual risk-taking behavior without much overarching theoretical integration or links with other problem behaviors. Yet as Jessor (1991) argued, any complete and responsible explanation of adolescent risk behavior needs to be complex and should incorporate multiple domains, including the social environment, the perceived environment, biology, and the interactions among multiple problem behaviors. It is critical that future research explores the impact of individually and contextually focused preventive interventions that target the core competencies. It is promising to see that an increasing number of interventions are beginning to address contextual influences such as race and neighborhood effects. Given the alarming racial health disparities in the United States, culturally competent programs, developed through empirical and theoretical research within affected communities, show promise in having a long-term effect on adolescent sexual risk behavior (Murry et al., 2007). Some of the literature has explored possible mediating effects of the core competencies in determining the risk association. However, largely missing from the literature is an exploration of the combination of core competencies as they relate to risky sexual behavior. For example, it is unknown whether it is a constellation of attributes with a direct impact on the behavior or if possessing or mastering a single one of the core competencies is enough to mitigate risk.

A research and intervention agenda that acknowledges the importance of individual characteristics of the adolescent while simultaneously acknowledging the complex and dynamic world in which adolescents live will contribute greatly to this already rich body of work. This agenda should focus on research that connects the core competencies to one another as well as the most salient contexts in youths' lives, including parents, peers, romantic relationships, schools, and neighborhoods. Additional research is needed to identify programs that help young people define their goals and connect their actions today with a desire to invest in their future. A promising prevention agenda is one that includes continual and early comprehensive information on sexual and reproductive health that is appropriate to the youth's developmental stage. Increased commitment to large-scale, longitudinal research and effective preventive intervention strategies is essential for reducing youth sexual risk taking.

References

Ajzen, I. (1991). The theory of planned behavior. *Organizational Behavior and Human Decision Processes, 50,* 179–211.

Ajzen, I., & Fishbein, M. (1980). *Understanding attitudes and predicting social behavior.* Upper Saddle River, NJ: Prentice Hall.

Albarracin, D., Johnson, B. T., Fishbein, M., & Muellerleile, P. A. (2001). Theories of reasoned action and planned behavior as models of condom use: A meta-analysis. *Psychological Bulletin, 127,* 142–161.

Aronowitz, T., Rennells, R. E., & Todd, E. (2006). Ecological influences of sexuality on early adolescent African American females. *Journal of Community Health Nursing, 23,* 113–122.

Bandura, A. (1977). *Social learning theory.* Upper Saddle River, NJ: Prentice Hall.

Blum, R. W., Beuhring, T., Shew, M. L., Bearinger, L. H., Sieving, R. E., & Resnick, M. D. (2000). The effects of race/ethnicity, income, and family structure on adolescent risk behaviors. *American Journal of Public Health, 90,* 1879–1884.

Brewster, K. L. (1994). Race differences in sexual activity among adolescent women: The role of neighborhood characteristics. *American Sociological Review, 59,* 408–424.

Bronfenbrenner, U. (1989). Ecological systems theory. *Annals of Child Development, 6,* 187–249.

Commendador, K. (2007). The relationship between female adolescent self-esteem, decision making, and contraceptive behavior. *Journal of the American Academy of Nurse Practitioners, 19,* 614–623.

Connolly, J. A., Connolly, J. A., & Konarski, R. (1994). Peer self-concept in adolescence: Analysis of factor structure and of associations with peer experience. *Journal of Research on Adolescence, 4,* 385–403.

Crane, J. (1991). Teen pregnancy as a function of high income workers in a community. *American Journal of Sociology, 96,* 1226–1259.

Crockett, L. J., Raffaelli, M., & Shen, Y. L. (2006). Linking self-regulation and risk proneness to risky sexual behavior: Pathways through peer pressure and early substance use. *Journal of Research on Adolescence, 16,* 503–525.

Crosby, R. A., DiClemente, R. J., Wingood, G. M., Cobb, B. K., Harrington, K., Davies, S. L., et al. (2001). HIV/STD-protective benefits of living with mothers in perceived supportive families: A study of high-risk African American female teens. *Preventive Medicine, 33,* 175–178.

Darroch, J., & Singh, S. (1999). *Why is teenage pregnancy declining? The roles of abstinence, sexual activity and contraceptive use.* New York: Guttmacher Institute.

DiClemente, R. J., Crosby, R. A., & Wingood, G. M. (2002). Enhancing STD/HIV prevention among adolescents: The importance of parental monitoring. *Minerva Pediatrica, 54,* 171–177.

DiClemente, R. J., Wingood, G. M., Crosby, R. A., Sionean, C., Brown, L. K., Rothbaum, B., et al. (2001). A prospective study of psychological distress and sexual risk behavior among Black adolescent females. *Pediatrics, 108,* E85.

Ethier, K. A., Kershaw, T. S., Lewis, J. B., Milan, S., Niccolai, L. M., & Ickovics, J. R. (2006). Self-esteem, emotional distress and sexual behavior among adolescent females: Inter-relationships and temporal effects. *Journal of Adolescent Health, 38,* 268–274.

Evans, A. E., Sanderson, M., Griffin, S. F., Reininger, B., Vincent, M. L., Parra-Medina, D., et al. (2004). An exploration of the relationship between youth assets and engagement in risky sexual behaviors. *Journal of Adolescent Health, 35,* 424–463.

Feldman, S. S., & Brown, N. L. (1993). Family influences on adolescent male sexuality: The mediational role of self-restraint. *Social Development, 2,* 15–35.

Fishbein, M., & Middlestadt, S. E. (1989). Using the theory of reasoned action as a framework for understanding and changing AIDS-related behaviors. In V. M. Mays, G. W. Albee, & S. S. Schneider (Eds.), *Primary prevention of AIDS: Psychological approaches* (pp. 93–110). Thousand Oaks, CA: Sage.

Furstenberg, F. F., Jr. (1987). Race differences in teenage sexuality, pregnancy, and adolescent childbearing. *Milbank Quarterly, 65*(Suppl. 2), 381–403.

Gardner, L. H., Frank, D., & Amankwaa, L. I. (1998). A comparison of sexual behavior and self-esteem in young adult females with positive and negative tests for sexually transmitted diseases. *Association of Black Nursing Faculty Journal, 9,* 89–94.

Geronimus, A. T. (2003). Damned if you do: Culture, identity, privilege, and teenage childbearing in the United States. *Social Science and Medicine, 57,* 881–893.

Guttmacher Institute. (2006). *Facts on sex education in the United States.* New York: Guttmacher Institute.

Guttmacher Institute. (2007). *U.S. teenage pregnancy statistics: National and state trends and trends by race and ethnicity.* Retrieved November 15, 2007, from http://www.guttmacher.org/pubs/2006/09/12/USTPstats.pdf.

Harlan, W. R., Harlan, E. A., & Grillo, G. P. (1980). Secondary sex characteristics of girls 12 to 17 years of age: The U.S. Health Examination Survey. *Journal of Pediatrics, 96,* 1074–1078.

Hart, B., & Hilton, I. (1988). Dimensions of personality organization as predictors of teenage pregnancy risk. *Journal of Personality Assessment, 52,* 116–133.

Harter, S., & Harter, S. (1999). *The construction of the self: A developmental perspective.* New York: Guilford Press.

Henrich, C. C., Brookmeyer, K. A., Shrier, L. A., & Shahar, G. (2006). Supportive relationships and sexual risk behavior in adolescence: An ecological-transactional approach. *Journal of Pediatric Psychology 31,* 286–297.

Hollen, P. J., & Hobbie, W. L. (1993). Risk taking and decision making of adolescent long-term survivors of cancer. *Oncology Nursing Forum, 20,* 769–776.

Hutchinson, M. K., Jemmott, J. B. III, Jemmott, L. S., Braverman, P., & Fong, G. T. (2003). The role of mother-daughter sexual risk communication in reducing sexual risk behaviors among urban adolescent females: A prospective study. *Journal of Adolescent Health, 33,* 98–107.

Hutchinson, M. K., & Wood, E. B. (2007). Reconceptualizing adolescent sexual risk in a parent-based expansion of the theory of planned behavior. *Journal of Nursing Scholarship, 39,* 141–146.

Jaccard, J., Dittus, P. J., & Gordon, V. V. (1998). Parent-adolescent congruency in reports of adolescent sexual behavior and in communications about sexual behavior. *Child Development, 69,* 247–261.

Jemmott, J. B., III, Heeren, G. A., Ngwane, Z., Hewitt, N., Jemmott, L. S., Shell, R., et al. (2007). Theory of planned behaviour predictors of intention to use condoms among Xhosa adolescents in South Africa. *AIDS Care, 19,* 677–684.

Jemmott, L. S., Jemmott, J. B. III, & Villarruel, A. M. (2002). Predicting intentions and condom use among Latino college students. *Journal of the Association of Nurses in AIDS Care, 13,* 59–69.

Jessor, R. (1991). Risk behavior in adolescence: A psychosocial framework for understanding and action. *Journal of Adolescent Health, 12,* 597–605.

Kirby, D. (2001). *Emerging answers: Research findings on programs to reduce teen pregnancy.* Washington, DC: National Campaign to Prevent Teen Pregnancy.

Kirby, D. (2002). Antecedents of adolescent initiation of sex, contraceptive use, and pregnancy. *American Journal of Health Behavior, 26,* 473–485.

Knauth, D. G., Skowron, E. A., & Escobar, M. (2006). Effect of differentiation of self on adolescent risk behavior: Test of the theoretical model. *Journal of Nursing Research, 55,* 336–345.

Kotchick, B. A., Shaffer, A., Forehand, R., & Miller, K. S. (2001). Adolescent sexual risk behavior: A multi-system perspective. *Clinical Psychology Review, 21,* 493–519.

Kowaleski-Jones, L., & Mott, F. L. (1998). Sex, contraception and childbearing among high-risk youth: Do different factors influence males and females? *Family Planning Perspectives, 30,* 163–169.

Ku, L., Sonenstein, F. L., & Pleck, J. H. (1993). Neighborhood, family, and work: Influences on the premarital behaviors of adolescent males. *Social Forces, 72,* 479–503.

Kuttler, A. F., Kuttler, A. F., La Greca, A. M., & Prinstein, M. J. (1999). Friendship qualities and social-emotional functioning of adolescents with close, cross-sex friendships. *Journal of Research on Adolescence, 9,* 339–366.

Luker, K. (1977). Contraceptive risk taking and abortion: Results and implications of a San Francisco Bay Area study. *Studies in Family Planning, 8,* 190–196.

Luster, T., & Small, S. A. (1994). Factors associated with sexual risk-taking behaviors among adolescents. *Journal of Marriage and the Family, 56,* 622–632.

Mann, L., Harmoni, R., & Power, C. (1989). Adolescent decision-making: The development of competence. *Journal of Adolescence, 12,* 265–278.

Masten, A. S., Coatsworth, J. D., Neemann, J., Gest, S. D., Tellegen, A., & Garmezy, N. (1995). The structure and coherence of competence from childhood through adolescence. *Child Development, 66,* 1635–1659.

McCree, D. H., Wingood, G. M., DiClemente, R., Davies, S., & Harrington, K. F. (2003). Religiosity and risky sexual behavior in African-American adolescent females. *Journal of Adolescent Health, 33,* 2–8.

McNair, L. D., Carter, J. A., & Williams, M. K. (1998). Self-esteem, gender, and alcohol use: Relationships with HIV risk perception and behaviors in college students. *Journal of Sex and Marital Therapy, 24,* 29–36.

Miller, K. S., Forehand, R., & Kotchick, B. A. (2000). Adolescent sexual behavior in two ethnic minority groups: A multisystem perspective. *Adolescence, 35,* 313–333.

Murry, V. M. (1996). An ecological analysis of coital timing among middle-class African American adolescent females. *Journal of Adolescent Research, 11,* 261–279.

Murry, V. M., Berkel, C., Brody, G. H., Gerrard, M., & Gibbons, F. X. (2007). The Strong African American Families program: Longitudinal pathways to sexual risk reduction. *Journal of Adolescent Health, 41,* 333–342.

Newcomer, S. F., & Udry, J. R. (1985). Parent-child communication and adolescent sexual behavior. *Family Planning Perspectives, 17*, 169–174.

O'Donnell, L., Stueve, A., O'Donnell, C., Duran, R., San Doval, A., Wilson, R., et al. (2002). Long-term reductions in sexual initiation and sexual activity among urban middle schoolers in the Reach for Health Service learning program. *Journal of Adolescent Health, 31*, 93–100.

O'Donnell, L., Stueve, A., San Doval, A., Duran, R., Haber, D., Atnafou, R., et al. (1999). The effectiveness of the Reach for Health Community Youth Service learning program in reducing early and unprotected sex among urban middle school students. *American Journal of Public Health, 89*, 176–181.

O'Sullivan, L. F., & Brooks-Gunn, J. (2005). The timing of changes in girls' sexual cognitions and behaviors in early adolescence: A prospective, cohort study. *Journal of Adolescent Health, 37*, 211–219.

Overby, K. J., & Kegeles, S. M. (1994). The impact of AIDS on an urban population of high-risk female minority adolescents: Implications for intervention. *Journal of Adolescent Health, 15*, 216–227.

Perrino, T., Gonzalez-Soldevilla, A., Pantin, H., & Szapocznik, J. (2000). The role of families in adolescent HIV prevention: A review. *Clinical Child and Family Psychology Review, 3*, 81–96.

Philliber, S., & Namerow, P. B. (1990). Using the Luker model to explain contraceptive use among adolescents. *Advances in Adolescent Mental Health, 4*, 71–86.

Raffaelli, M., & Crockett, L. J. (2003). Sexual risk taking in adolescence: The role of self-regulation and attraction to risk. *Developmental Psychology, 39*, 1036–1046.

Reitman, D., St. Lawrence, J. S., Jefferson, K. W., Alleyne, E., Brasfield, T. L., & Shirley, A. (1996). Predictors of African American adolescents' condom use and HIV risk behavior. *AIDS Education and Prevention, 8*, 499–515.

Resnick, M. D., Bearman, P. S., Blum, R. W., Bauman, K. E., Harris, K. M., Jones, J., et al. (1997). Protecting adolescents from harm: Findings from the National Longitudinal Study on Adolescent Health. *Journal of American Medical Association, 278*, 823–832.

Rodgers, J. L., Rodgers, J. L., & Rowe, D. C. (1990). Adolescent sexual activity and mildly deviant behavior: Sibling and friendship effects. *Journal of Family Issues, 11*, 274–293.

Salazar, L. F., DiClemente, R. J., Wingood, G. M., Crosby, R. A., Harrington, K., Davies, S., et al. (2004). Self-concept and adolescents' refusal of unprotected sex: A test of mediating mechanisms among African American girls. *Prevention Science, 5*, 137–149.

Santelli, J. S., Lindberg, L. D., Finer, L. B., & Singh, S. (2007). Explaining recent declines in adolescent pregnancy in the United States: The contribution of abstinence and improved contraceptive use. *American Journal of Public Health, 97*, 150–156.

Scaramella, L. V., Conger, R. D., Simons, R. L., & Whitbeck, L. B. (1998). Predicting risk for pregnancy by late adolescence: A social contextual perspective. *Developmental Psychology, 34*, 1233–1245.

Sinha, J. W., Cnaan, R. A., & Gelles, R. J. (2007). Adolescent risk behaviors and religion: Findings from a national study. *Journal of Adolescence, 30*, 231–249.

Tosh, A. K., & Simmons, P. S. (2007). Sexual activity and other risk-taking behaviors among Asian-American adolescents. *Journal of Pediatric and Adolescent Gynecology, 20*, 29–34.

Trenholm, C., Devaney, B., Fortson, K., Quay, L., Wheeler, J., & Clark, M. (2007). *Impacts of four Title V, Section 510 abstinence education programs: Final report.* Princeton, NJ: Mathematica.

Villarruel, A. M., Jemmott, J. B. III, Jemmott, L. S., & Ronis, D. L. (2004). Predictors of sexual intercourse and condom use intentions among Spanish-dominant Latino youth: A test of the planned behavior theory. *Nursing Research, 53*, 172–181.

Weinstock, H., Berman, S., & Cates, W., Jr. (2004). Sexually transmitted diseases among American youth: Incidence and prevalence estimates, 2000. *Perspectives on Sexual and Reproductive Health, 36,* 6–10.

Whitbeck, L. B., Whitbeck, L. B., Conger, R. D., Simons, R. L., & Kao, M. (1993). Minor deviant behaviors and adolescent sexual activity. *Youth and Society, 25,* 24–37.

Wickrama, K.A.S., Merten, M. J., & Elder, G. H. (2005). Community influences on precocious transitions to adulthood: Racial differences and mental health consequences. *Journal of Community Psychology, 33*(6), 639–653.

Yang, H., Stanton, B., Li, X., Cottrel, L., Galbraith, J., & Kaljee, L. (2007). Dynamic association between parental monitoring and communication and adolescent risk involvement among African-American adolescents. *Journal of the National Medical Association, 99,* 517–524.

VIGNETTA EUGENIA CHARLES is a doctoral candidate in the Department of Population, Family and Reproductive Health at the Johns Hopkins Bloomberg School of Public Health.

ROBERT WM. BLUM is the William H. Gates Sr. Professor and chair of the Department of Population, Family and Reproductive Health at the Johns Hopkins Bloomberg School of Public Health.

Naudeau, S., Cunningham, W., Lundberg, M.K.A., & McGinnis, L. (2008). Programs and policies that promote positive youth development and prevent risky behaviors: An international perspective. In N. G. Guerra & C. P. Bradshaw (Eds.), *Core competencies to prevent problem behaviors and promote positive youth development. New Directions for Child and Adolescent Development, 122,* 75–87.

6

Programs and Policies That Promote Positive Youth Development and Prevent Risky Behaviors: An International Perspective

Sophie Naudeau, Wendy Cunningham, Mattias K. A. Lundberg, Linda McGinnis

Abstract

This chapter provides an international perspective on the promotion of positive development and the prevention of risky behavior among youth. We discuss some of the specific challenges that youth face in low- and middle-income countries and identify six key evidence-based policies and programs that aim to promote positive youth development and prevent risky behavior. We also propose a set of practical recommendations for policymakers and other stakeholders on how to develop and implement an effective youth portfolio in the context of limited financial resources. © Wiley Periodicals, Inc.

This chapter is a product of the staff of the International Bank for Reconstruction and Development/The World Bank. The findings, interpretations, and conclusions expressed in this chapter do not necessarily reflect the views of the executive directors of the World Bank or the governments they represent.

There are currently 1.5 billion people between the ages of twelve and twenty-four worldwide, with 1.3 billion of them living in developing countries—the most ever in history. Youth require specific policy attention not only because they are so numerous but also because they must navigate many of life's crucial transitions in a short time (World Bank, 2007a). These transitions include going from school to work, forming families, taking responsibilities for their own health, and becoming full citizens (World Bank, 2006). Failure to navigate these transitions in a productive and timely manner is often manifest in risky behaviors such as those described in previous chapters of this volume and can have dire repercussions for both individuals and their society.

This may be particularly true for youth living in poverty or who are otherwise disadvantaged based on family background, minority status, disability, or even gender, depending on the context. These youth are often labeled as "at risk" because they face environmental, social, and family conditions that hinder their personal development and their successful integration into society as productive citizens (World Bank, 2003). Compared to other youth, they tend to have a greater propensity to engage in risky behaviors such as school absenteeism and dropping out, sexual behaviors potentially leading to early pregnancy or HIV/AIDS (or both), delinquency, violence, and substance use and abuse. Because the negative outcomes of such behaviors are extremely costly to societies, policymakers worldwide tend to focus on youth only when or after problems arise (Cunningham, McGinnis, Teliuc, Garcia-Verdu, & Verner, 2008).

Yet once a young person has began to engage in risky behaviors and to experience negative outcomes, the means by which he or she can recover and return to a safe, positive, and productive path of development are often challenging and costly. Therefore, rather than trying to contain or alleviate the damaging consequences of risky behaviors after the fact, it is usually more beneficial to youth, and more cost-effective for societies, to promote the positive development of young people from an early start by equipping them with the skills or competences they need to successfully manage the transition to adulthood (Cunningham, Cohan, Naudeau, & McGinnis, 2008).

This shift from a deficit perspective that sees youth as problems to be managed to a positive youth development approach that views youth as resources to be developed is grounded in a burgeoning body of literature and research that empirically validates what parents, practitioners, and youth themselves have experienced and observed all along: a successful transition to adulthood requires much more than simply staying away from drugs, alcohol, early sexual activity, violence, and other risk behaviors (Eccles & Gootman, 2002; Lerner et al., 2005; Roth & Brooks-Gunn, 2003). It requires that youth be equipped with a number of positive attributes and skills or competencies. This chapter provides examples and suggestions for nurturing these competencies in young people from various backgrounds across the world, so that they can lead happy and productive adult lives while simultaneously avoiding risky behavior.

Promoting the Positive Development of Youth in Developing Countries

This section describes some of the most effective policies and interventions that can be implemented in various regions of the world in order to promote the positive development of young people from an early start and to prevent them from engaging in behavior that puts their human capital, or even their lives, at risk. It is also important to acknowledge that adolescence and early adulthood is a time of identity formation, brain development, and experimentation, during which a certain amount of risk taking can be considered normative and even developmentally appropriate. In addition, many youth, especially in developing countries, grow up in conditions of devastating poverty and social exclusion that expose them to additional risks and challenges. Accordingly, this section also includes recommendations for policies and programs that can help limit the negative consequences of risky behaviors when they do occur in order to help young people recover to a healthy developmental path.

Though interrelated, these six key policy and program recommendations can be categorized as follows: (1) start with the family: provide health care and parenting information and support to expecting and new parents; (2) foster connections to school from an early age and for as long as possible; (3) incorporate life skills into all interventions for youth; (4) develop youth-friendly reproductive health services; (5) provide youth with opportunities for civic engagement; and (6) provide youth with information and guidance. It is important to note, however, that while these recommended programs and practices are expected to be effective across a wide range of cultures and contexts, the specific means through which they should be implemented will vary from place to place, and some adaptations may be necessary to optimize the contextual fit.

Start with the Family: Provide Parenting Information and Support to Expecting and New Parents. Parenting programs can have immediate effects on the positive development of teenage parents (through better decision-making skills, among others) and long-term effects on the healthy and adaptive development of their children across domains: cognitive competence, social connectedness, emotional regulation and self-control, and physical development. Evidence from studies in the Caribbean, Brazil, Honduras, Mexico, and Chile suggests that low self-esteem and feelings of rage in young people can be traced back to the home: maternal emotional abandonment, the absence of parental nurturing, unskilled parents, sexual abuse, and being part of an aggressive family (Cunningham et al., 2008). Research indicates that youth who feel connected to their parents and receive the appropriate types and amounts of discipline, as well as moral guidance, demonstrate higher levels of self-control, conflict resolution, peer resistance, and overall psychosocial adjustment; and they in turn are less prone to emotional distress, suicidal thoughts and attempts, school failure, drug and alcohol abuse, violent behavior, and early sexual activity (Blum & Rinehart, 1997; Gomby, Culross, & Behrman, 1999).

As an example, an evaluation of the Mother-Child Education Program in Turkey showed greater educational attainment and reduced delinquency among participating children and an increased sense of empowerment among participating young mothers (Kagitcibasi, Sunar, & Bekman, 2001). Responsive and interactive parenting can also offset many of the adverse consequences of childhood malnutrition on cognitive development, as documented in the Philippines and other contexts (Pan-American Health Organization, 2005; World Bank, 2006).

Parenting training, which usually includes information about proper care, nutrition, stimulation, and discipline, can be a separate intervention or a component of a comprehensive, multiservice program. The most common types of parenting training programs in the developing world consist of home visits, which target families with infants aged up to three years old and are usually offered in the context of comprehensive early child development programs that also include center-based activities for preschool age children. The visits typically are conducted by a nurse or other trained professional who goes to the homes of expecting and new mothers and fathers to provide them with parenting training and counseling. The main goal of these visits is to promote healthy child development, including prosocial connectedness and positive sense of self, by influencing parents' attitudes, knowledge, and behavior as well as to prevent child abuse and neglect. Other goals may include improving the overall family environment by providing parents with job placement assistance and encouragement to continue their education or delay further childbearing.

Investing in family-based parenting training is one of the most cost-effective ways to promote the positive development of children and youth and prevent risky behavior, particularly among families in which parents have low education levels or live in poverty. In addition, many first-time parents in developing countries are still teenagers themselves, which means that they must navigate simultaneously the sometimes conflicting demands of youth and of parenthood. Parenting information and support is particularly useful for these young parents, who may struggle with many transitions at once. Evidence further indicates that the earlier these interventions are implemented and the longer they last, the greater the benefits they yield (Cunningham et al., 2008).

Foster Connections to Schools from an Early Age and for as Long as Possible. Today many developing countries are getting close to achieving universal primary completion, but most countries continue to face enormous challenges in ensuring access to schooling opportunities for both younger and older children through preschool services and secondary education, respectively, and in promoting quality education and good learning outcomes (Mullis, Martin, Kennedy, & Foy, 2007). Schooling can foster the positive development of youth in two interrelated ways: first, through the knowledge and skills that children and youth acquire when benefiting from quality education, which increase their chance to manage a successful school-to-work transition and enable them to make more informed decisions, particularly in regard to sexual and reproductive health; second, through the sense of connectedness that students often feel with peers and adults in their school (Cunningham et al., 2008). Studies in Brazil, the Caribbean, Mexico, Honduras, and Chile show that when students feel connected to their schools, they are more likely to be motivated and engaged in the classroom, perform academically, and complete their education, and less likely to skip school, fight, or engage in bullying and vandalism (Blum, 2006, Cunningham et al., 2008).

Investing in the education of children and youth from an early age and throughout adolescence is one of the most important investments a country can make to promote the educational outcomes and decision-making skills of young people and reduce nearly all kinds of risky behaviors (U.S. Surgeon General, 2001). Providing young children with developmentally appropriate stimulation before primary school is particularly important and effective given that significant brain development occurs within the first five years of life. The stimulation that the brain receives during these early years greatly influences cognitive and linguistic development as well as social and psychological skills and behavior later in life, such as decision-making skills, self-control, and a positive sense of self (Shonkoff & Phillips, 2000). A child's environment and early experiences determine lifelong trajectories and abilities for learning, behavior, and health. In addition to providing information to parents of young children, quality early child development programs usually include center-based activities for preschool-age children (those three to five years old) through the formal school system or community-based programs run by trained teachers.

The effects of preschool education on behavioral patterns in later life are well documented worldwide. In the United States, evaluations of the High/Scope Perry Preschool Project have demonstrated that young people and adults born into poverty who participated in high-quality preschool programs committed fewer crimes, had higher earnings, were more likely to hold a job, and were more likely to have graduated from high school than those who did not participate (Schweinhart et al., 2005). In low- and middle-income countries, participation in preschool activities has been linked to less grade repetition and lower dropout rates, higher school attainment and completion, improved attention, better learning outcomes, and increased exposure to the official schooling language (Berlinski, Galiani, & Gertler, 2006; Grantham-McGregor et al., 2007; Vegas & Petrow, 2008). In Brazil, a study of the impact of preschool showed a benefit-cost ratio of two-to-one for children who attended one year of preschool, as well as a delay in the age of first pregnancy among female participants (World Bank, 2001).

At the secondary level, examples of policies that have been successful in improving enrollment and completion rates, particularly when combined with one another, include providing financial incentives (for example, conditional cash transfers, school vouchers, loans, grants, individual learning accounts, school supplies, and free public transportation) targeted to poor or otherwise disadvantaged youth in order to increase the demand for secondary school and offset competing demands such as work and child care; improving the quality and relevance of secondary education to increase the ability of youth to successfully manage their school-to-work transition; and providing options such as education equivalency for school dropouts so that they can complete high school and enter tertiary education or the labor market (Cunningham et al., 2008).

Studies have documented the positive impacts of education equivalency programs (flexible programs that provide youth who dropped out of school with the opportunity to earn a degree) on school completion and labor market participation rates in Chile (Guerra, 2006) and Trinidad and Tobago. It is anticipated that several of the core competencies mediate these positive outcomes, such as better social and interaction skills, increased confidence and self-esteem, a higher sense of self-efficacy over their lives, the ability to seek out new opportunities, and a sense of connectedness with peers, teachers, and schools (Saunders, Jones, Bowman, Loveder, & Brooks, 2003; Wyn, Stokes, & Tyler, 2004).

Incorporate Life Skills into All Interventions for Youth. Although not uniformly defined, life skills (sometimes known as soft skills) fall into three basic categories: (1) social or interpersonal skills (which may include communication, negotiation and refusal skills, assertiveness, cooperation, and empathy); (2) cognitive skills (problem solving, understanding sequences, decision making, critical thinking, and self-evaluation); and (3) emotional coping skills (including a positive sense of self) and self-control (managing stress, feelings, and moods) (Pan American Health Organization, 2005). Teaching life skills can promote positive development and widen the scope of opportunities available to all young people. This is particularly true for youth who have not had a chance to learn these skills at home or through connections with positive role models and for those who left school early and are typically less likely to find quality employment.

Evaluations from around the world have found that life skills training programs can lead to improved academic performance, improved social judgment, better anger management, and less drug use and risky sexual behavior among youth (Mangrulkar, Whitman, & Posner, 2001). Life skills can be taught through schools, job training institutions, or a learning-by-doing approach, for example, as part of community development projects or youth leadership training programs (Hahn, Leavitt, & Lanspery, 2006).

Develop Youth-Friendly Reproductive Health Services. Reproductive health services include support during pregnancy, such as prenatal, postpartum, and abortion services, as well as prevention and health promotion. In addition, services targeted to youth may include providing information and counseling on sexuality, safe sex, sexual violence and abuse, and referral for any needed services (Senderowitz, 1999).

The World Health Organization estimates that more than 1 million cases of sexually transmitted infections (STIs), including HIV/AIDS, occur each day, with the highest infection rates among those fifteen to twenty-four years old (Dehne & Riedner, 2005). Most are easily treated, without severe or lasting consequences, if diagnosed and treated early. But unmarried adolescents are often denied services in countries where premarital sex is frowned upon. In some places, young married women are refused services if they cannot demonstrate the consent of their spouses (Stanback & Twum-Baah, 2001). Even where young people are legally protected, many obstacles prevent youth from using existing services, including inconvenient hours, lack of transportation, high costs, lack of information about their existence, fears about the lack of confidentiality, or cultural and gender barriers (Cunningham et al., 2008). For these reasons, making clinics youth-friendly by training doctors and nurses on how to interact with young clients, having clinic hours that are convenient for youth, and offering space where young people can consult with providers in privacy may increase the use of health services among young people.

Several types of interventions have been shown to be particularly effective in increasing young people's use of reproductive health services in a wide range of developing country settings. These include training service providers and other clinic and pharmaceutical staff in youth-friendly practices; making clinics and pharmacies more accessible and acceptable to young people, for example, by providing services in mobile units to visit poor and rural areas; and using community-based outreach and information campaigns to generate both demand and support for reproductive health services among young people. Evaluations of such interventions in Mexico, Brazil, Nigeria, South Africa, and Madagascar have found increased knowledge about the specific needs of young people among trained health professionals and changes in decision-making processes and outcomes among youth, as documented by increased use of reproductive health services, higher rates of contraceptive use (including condoms), and longer periods of breastfeeding among teenage mothers (Martin, Schenkl, & Vernon, 1992; Okonofua et al., 2003; Population Services International, 2004; Shepard, Garcia-Nunez, & Miller, 1989; Transgrud, 1998; Wolfe, 2005).

Provide Youth with Opportunities for Civic Engagement. Youth civic engagement offers the opportunity for young people to play an active role in their community, while at the same time learning new skills, increasing their employability, and contributing to their overall personal development (Lerner, 2004; Sherrod, Flanagan, & Youniss, 2002). Studies have shown that participation in civic activities can foster increased self-esteem and confidence and a greater sense of inclusion and empowerment among youth, while at the same time reducing their propensity to engage in risky behaviors such as drugs and alcohol abuse, delinquent behavior, and dropping out of school (Alessi, 2004; McBride, Olate, & Johnson, 2008; Perry, 2003).

In practice, programs that promote civic engagement or service among youth typically require them to make a voluntary commitment of time and effort to activities that contribute to the development of their local, national, or global community (Sherraden, 2001). They can be run by governments, employers, nonprofit organizations, and other civil society groups and may include services such as volunteering in public health clinics, building sustainable housing, literacy tutoring, protecting the environment, or building small-scale infrastructure. Youth service programs are more likely to be successful if they provide structured, organized activities and sustained participation by each young person (Cunningham et al., 2008).

Provide Youth with Information and Guidance. Finally, allowing young people to make positive choices across developmental domains such as education, employment, and family formation and to avoid engaging in risky behavior requires providing them with information and guidance. Youth are not merely passive beneficiaries of services such as education and health. As they move from childhood to adulthood, they become increasingly independent decision makers who must choose from a wide array of available options with widely varying consequences. In the absence of information and guidance, the range of perceived or real positive and relevant options may narrow, and youth may be more likely to engage in the only options that seem available to them: low-quality alternatives or risky behaviors, or both (World Bank, 2006, 2007a). Youth may have biased views about the value of education, for instance, as shown in a survey of boys in the Dominican Republic who severely underestimated the economic returns to completing secondary school (Jensen, 2006). Boys who were given the true returns were significantly more likely to attend school the following year than those who did not receive the information. Youth may also have distorted expectations of the type of employment they can secure, or they may not fully understand the repercussions of early marriage or the possible consequences of drug use.

Both the school context and the media can be effective ways to inform youth about existing opportunities available to them (for example, financial assistance, health services, employment services) and to expose them to positive messages and role models. Schools have several advantages as a place for delivering information and guidance. Specifically, schools reach many young people at once from an early age, and they are responsible for imparting skills and knowledge in a structured and safe environment. In addition, teachers whom youth perceive as caring and trustworthy can act as positive role models (Cunningham et al., 2008). This is especially important in the delivery of information on sensitive topics such as sexuality (Blum, 2006).

Positive messages and role modeling can also be delivered through radio, TV, print, the Internet, and other media and are an effective way to reach youth, particularly those who have dropped out of school and are therefore not able to benefit from school-based programs (Cunningham et al., 2008). Social marketing campaigns have been shown to equip youth with the knowledge and skills needed to increase their self-efficacy, improve their decision-making skills, and resist peer pressure or other incentives to engage in risky behavior in a number of developing countries, including Cameroon, Paraguay, and Tanzania (Plautz & Meekers, 2007; Population Services International, 2002; World Health Organization, 2006). This is particularly true when media campaigns provide youth not only with information about what to do or not to do, but also concrete advice about where to find the services they may need, such as career orientation services, free condoms, or counseling.

Using Scarce Resources Efficiently

The policy and program recommendations discussed here are not meant to be exhaustive. They are merely the policies for which the strongest evidence of effectiveness is available. Additional approaches may be worth pursuing, but must be justified on the basis of rigorous evidence. A number of popular policies and programs intended to promote positive youth development and prevent risky behavior have, however, been found to be either ineffective or even harmful. These include boot camps and other get-tough programs (treating juvenile offenders as adults), zero tolerance or shock programs (programs that aim to "shock" students through exposing them to the negative effects of risky behaviors), gun buy-back programs (except possibly in the context of postconflict environments), grade repetition without adequate remedial support, abstinence-only programs, and building youth centers without commensurate support for the training of facilitators (Cunningham et al., 2008a, 2008b). These approaches are often politically popular, appealing quick fixes for complex problems. Yet where resources are scarce, investments must be made on the basis of demonstrated impact and relative cost-effectiveness.

In addition, budgetary constraints often preclude governments in developing countries from investing in programs and policies that target all children and youth. For instance, universal preschool may be ideal, but there is a strong public good rationale for focusing public resources on poor or otherwise disadvantaged children. Indeed, steep socioeconomic gradients in developmental outcomes have been documented among young children throughout the world (Grantham-McGregor et al., 2007), mostly because wealthier children already have access to family resources and private services. Public investments in the development of disadvantaged children are likely to yield greater social benefits than public investments among the wealthy, which would merely substitute for existing private investment.

The Way Forward: Measuring Positive Development Among Youth in Low- and Middle-Income Countries

This chapter provides examples of programs and policies that have been effective in promoting positive development and reducing risky behavior among youth in a number of settings. However, youth and governments alike face different challenges and constraints across contexts and cultures, and the optimal portfolio of effective youth policies and programs will vary accordingly. Consequently, the findings presented here may have limited external validity.

Youth programs and policies must be evaluated rigorously to yield information for policymakers and other stakeholders for terminating, modifying, or scaling up specific interventions. The lessons learned from these evaluations must be widely disseminated to promote transparency and dialogue among various actors, including youth. Rigorous, well-controlled evaluations can be expensive, and officials may be reluctant to spend their scarce resources on evaluating a program rather than on investing these resources in the program itself. Yet failing to invest in evaluation can be shortsighted and self-defeating if it means that poorly performing programs are continued and that lessons cannot be applied to future interventions (see Cunningham et al., 2008; World Bank, 2007b). In addition, programs and policies for youth must be chosen on the basis of greatest cost-effectiveness and positive net benefit. Indeed, the interventions discussed in this chapter are usually implemented by public agencies, and these agencies have an obligation to invest public resources as effectively and efficiently as possible.

The need for rigorous impact evaluations begs the question of how to measure success. Successful interventions must reduce the prevalence of risky behavior among youth but should also aim to nurture the core attributes or competencies that help youth successfully navigate the transition to adulthood. This also has implications for monitoring. Indeed, data are often collected on the prevalence of youth risky behaviors, but rarely on measures of positive youth development such as those included in the Five Cs model (Lerner et al., 2005) or in the core competencies framework discussed in this volume.

Here, lessons can be learned from the process of measuring developmental outcomes such as school readiness among preschool-aged children worldwide. Indeed, several of the measurement tools now available for this young age group reflect the fact that the absence of behavioral problems, for instance, should not necessarily be taken as an indication of social and emotional wellbeing (Fernald, Raikes, & Dean, 2006). Similarly, what the field of youth development needs is a measure of readiness for the many challenges of early adulthood, including school-to-work transition, family formation, and citizenship, that includes an assessment of competencies or strengths. These indicators must measure our efforts and success in providing opportunities and guidance, not only to the majority of young people in the United States and Europe who complete secondary school, but also to the majority of young people in the developing world who do not. Every one of these young people must be afforded the chance to negotiate the transition to a happy, healthy, and productive adulthood.

References

Alessi, B. (2004). *Service as a strategy for children and youth.* Washington, DC: Innovations in Civic Participation.

Berlinski, S., Galiani, S., & Gertler, P. (2006). *The effect of pre-primary education on primary school performance.* Ann Arbor: University of Michigan, William Davidson Institute, Stephen M. Ross Business School.

Blum, R. W. (2006). *Policy and program recommendations in adolescent sexual and reproductive health for Latin America and the Caribbean.* Washington, DC: World Bank.

Blum, R. W., & Rinehart, P. (1997). *Reducing the risk: Connections that make a difference in the lives of youth.* Minneapolis: University of Minnesota, Division of General Pediatrics and Adolescent Health.

Cunningham, W., Cohan, L., Naudeau, S., & McGinnis, L. (2008a). *Supporting youth at risk: A policy toolkit for middle-income countries.* Washington, DC: World Bank.

Cunningham, W., McGinnis, L., Teliuc, C., Garcia-Verdu, R., & Verner, D. (2008b). *The promise of youth: Policies for youth at risk in Latin America and the Caribbean.* Washington, DC: World Bank.

Dehne, K. L., & Riedner, G. (2005). *Sexually transmitted infections among adolescents: The need for adequate health services.* Geneva: World Health Organization.

Eccles, J., & Gootman, J. (Eds.). (2002). *Community programs to promote youth development.* Washington, DC: National Academy Press.

Fernald, L., Raikes, A., & Dean, R. (2006). *Summary of child development assessments and applications to evaluations in the developing world.* Washington, DC: World Bank.

Gomby, D., Culross, P., & Behrman, R. (1999). Home visiting: Recent program evaluations—analysis and recommendations. *Future of Children, 9,* 4–26.

Grantham-McGregor, S., Bun Cheung, Y., Cueto, S., Glewwe, P., Richer, L., Trupp, B., et al. (2007). Developmental potential in the first 5 years for children in developing countries. *Lancet, 369,* 60–70.

Guerra, N. G. (2006). *Youth at risk in Latin America and the Caribbean: Preventing violence and crime—policy recommendations.* Washington, DC: World Bank.

Hahn, A., Leavitt, T., & Lanspery, S. (2006). *Toward a toolkit brief: The importance of life skills training to assist vulnerable groups of youth in the Latin America and Caribbean Region.* Washington, DC: World Bank.

Jensen, R. (2006). *Do the perceived returns to education affect schooling decisions? Evidence from a randomized Experiment.* Cambridge, MA: Harvard University, John F. Kennedy School of Government.

Kagitcibasi, C., Sunar, D., & Bekman, S. (2001). Long-term effect of early intervention: Turkish low-income mothers and children. *Applied Developmental Psychology, 22,* 333–361.

Lerner, R. M. (2004). *Liberty: Thriving and civic engagement among American youth.* Thousand Oaks, CA: Sage.

Lerner, R. M., Lerner, J. V., Almerigi, J., Theokas, C., Phelps, E., Gestsdottir, S., et al. (2005). Positive youth development, participation in community youth development programs, and community contributions of fifth grade adolescents: Findings from the first wave of the 4-H Study of Positive Youth Development. *Journal of Early Adolescence, 25,* 17–71.

Mangrulkar, L., Whitman, C., & Posner, M. (2001). *Life skills approach to child and adolescent healthy human development.* Retrieved March 3, 2008, from http://www.paho.org/English/HPP/HPF/ADOL/Lifeskills.pdf.

Martin, A., Schenkel, P., & Vernon, R. (1992, June). *A sustainable educational program for postpartum adolescent mothers, Mexico.* Paper presented at the annual National Council of International Health Conference, Arlington, VA.

McBride, A. M., Olate, R., & Johnson, L. (2008). *Youth volunteer service in Latin America and the Caribbean: A regional assessment* St. Louis, MO: Washington University, Center for Social Development.

Mullis, I., Martin, M., Kennedy, A., & Foy, P. (2007). *PIRLS 2006 international report.* Boston: Boston College, Lynch School of Education, IEA TIMSS and PIRLS International Study Center.

Okonofua, F. E., Coplan, P., Collins, S., Oronsaye, F., Ogunsakin, D., Ogonor, J. T., et al. (2003). Impact of an intervention to improve treatment-seeking behavior and prevent sexually transmitted diseases among Nigerian youths. *International Journal of Infectious Diseases, 7,* 61–73.

Pan American Health Organization. (2005). *Youth: Choices and change. Promoting healthy behavior in adolescents.* Washington, DC: Author.

Perry, J. (2003). *Civic service: What difference does it make?* Armonk, NY: M. E. Sharpe.

Plautz, A., & Meekers, D. (2007). Evaluation of the reach and impact of the 100% Jeune youth social marketing program in Cameroon: Findings from three cross-sectional surveys. *Reproductive Health, 4,* 1–15.

Population Services International. (2002, January). Adolescent health project makes waves in Paraguay. *PSI: Social Marketing and Communications for Health Profile.* Retrieved March 4, 2008, from http://www.psi.org/resources/pubs/ArteyParte.pdf.

Population Services International. (2004, August). *Franchised youth clinics motivate behavior change in Madagascar.* Washington, DC: Author.

Roth, J. L., & Brooks-Gunn, J. (2003). What exactly is a youth development program? Answers from research and practice. *Applied Developmental Science, 7,* 94–111

Saunders, J., Jones, M., Bowman, K., Loveder, P., & Brooks, L. (2003). *Indigenous people in vocational education and training: A statistical review of progress.* Retrieved March 10, 2008, from www.ncver.edu.au/research/commercial/op298.pdf.

Schweinhart, L. J., Montie, J., Xiang, Z. Barnett, W. S. Belfied, C. B., & Nores, M. (2005). *Lifetime effects: The High/Scope Perry Preschool study through age 40.* Ypsilanti, MI: High/Scope Press.

Senderowitz, J. (1999). *Making reproductive health services youth friendly.* Retrieved March 30, 2008 from http://www.pathfind.org/focus.htm.

Shepard, B. L., Garcia-Nunez, J., & Miller, J. T. (1989, November). *Adolescent program approaches in Latin America and the Caribbean: An overview of implementation and evaluation issues.* Paper presented to the International Conference in Adolescent Fertility in Latin America and the Caribbean, Oaxaca, Mexico.

Sherraden, M. (2001). *Youth service as strong policy.* Working paper. St. Louis, MO: Washington University, Center for Social Development.

Sherrod, L., Flanagan, C., & Youniss, J. (2002). Growing into citizenship: Multiple pathways and diverse influence. *Applied Developmental Science, 6,* 264–272.

Shonkoff, J., & Phillips, D. (2000). *From neurons to neighborhoods: The science of early childhood development.* Washington, DC: National Academy Press.

Stanback, J., & Twum-Baah, K. A. (2001). Why do family planning providers restrict access to services? An examination in Ghana. *International Family Planning Perspectives, 27,* 37–41.

Trangsrud, R. (1998). *Adolescent reproductive health in east and southern Africa: Building experience, four case studies.* Nairobi, Kenya: Regional Adolescent Reproductive Health Network.

U.S. Surgeon General. (2001). *Youth violence: A report of the surgeon general.* Washington, DC: U.S. Department of Health and Human Services.

Vegas, E., & Petrow, J. (in press). *Raising student learning in Latin America: The challenge for the 21st century.* Washington, DC: World Bank.

Wolfe, K. (2005). *Youth friendly pharmacies and partnerships: The CMS-CELSAM experience.* Bethesda, MD: Private Sector Partnerships-One Project.

World Bank. (2001). *Brazil early child development: A focus on the impact of preschool.* Washington, DC: Author.

World Bank. (2003). *Caribbean youth development: Issues and policy directions.* Washington, DC: Author.

World Bank. (2006). *World development report 2007: Development and the next generation.* New York: Author.

World Bank. (2007a). *Youth: An undervalued asset: Towards a new agenda in the Middle East and North Africa. Progress, challenges, and way forward.* Washington DC: Author.

World Bank. (2007b). Evaluating youth interventions. *Youth Development Notes, 11,* 1–4. Retrieved March 2, 2008, from http://siteresources.worldbank.org/INTCY/Resources/395766-1186420121500/YDNVolII5Evaluation.pdf. .

World Health Organization. (2006). *Preventing HIV/AIDS in young people: A systematic review of the evidence from developing countries* (D. A. Ross, B. Dick, & J. Ferguson, Eds.). Geneva, Switzerland: Author.

Wyn, J., Stokes, H., and Tyler, D. (2004). *Stepping stones: TAFE and ACE program development for early school leavers.* National Centre for Vocational Education Research. Stational Arcade, Adelaide, Australia. Retrieved March 10, 2008, from http://www.ncver.edu.au/publications/index.html.

SOPHIE NAUDEAU *is a human development specialist at the World Bank, Washington, D.C.*

WENDY CUNNINGHAM *is a senior economist at the World Bank, Washington, D.C.*

MATTIAS K. A. LUNDBERG *is a senior economist at the World Bank, Washington, D.C.*

LINDA MCGINNIS *is a lead economist at the World Bank, Washington, D.C.*

Bradshaw, C. P., & Guerra, N. G. (2008). Future directions for research on core competencies. In N. G. Guerra & C. P. Bradshaw (Eds.), *Core competencies to prevent problem behaviors and promote positive youth development. New Directions for Child and Adolescent Development*, 122, 89–92.

Future Directions for Research on Core Competencies

Catherine P. Bradshaw, Nancy G. Guerra

Abstract

This concluding commentary highlights common themes that emerged across the chapters in this volume. We identify strengths and limitations of the core competencies framework and discuss the importance of context, culture, and development for understanding the role of the core competencies in preventing risk behavior in adolescence. We also outline possible areas for future research linking positive youth development and risk prevention programming. © Wiley Periodicals, Inc.

Throughout this volume, a primary aim has been to highlight connections between youth development approaches that emphasize strengths for all youth and risk-prevention approaches that identify deficits related to specific problem behaviors. As we noted at the outset, these approaches often have been cast as opposite ends of a continuum. Advocates of positive youth development endorse asset-building strategies to promote healthy adjustment, noting that youth who are "problem free" are not necessarily thriving or prepared to make the transition from adolescence to adulthood (Pittman, Irby, Tolman, Yohalem, & Ferber, 2003). Supporters of risk prevention emphasize the damaging consequences of problem behaviors for adolescents and the communities they grow up in. Because empirical studies have identified specific factors that increase the likelihood of each type of problem behavior, preventive efforts that target these risk factors should be more effective and ultimately less costly to society. Indeed, as Naudeau, Cunningham, Lundberg, and McGinnis discussed in Chapter Six, policies and programs must be sensitive to the realities of limited financial resources in the United States and internationally.

An important next step is to integrate the risk-prevention literature around common themes (translate risk, protective, and promotive factors) and to build bridges between youth development and risk-prevention approaches in order to specify more clearly common predictors of multiple problem behaviors and how these are linked to healthy adjustment. Our primary focus in this volume has been to identify common predictors of four distinct problem behaviors: early school leaving, youth violence, adolescent substance use, and high-risk sexual behavior. This proved to be a reasonably difficult task, in part because each type of problem behavior tends to generate its own nomenclature for describing predictors, and there are often inconsistencies in how researchers label common constructs. For example, in examining how youth make decisions and think about consequences, substance use researchers emphasize "decision-making skills," whereas violence researchers examine "social problem solving" or "social information processing skills." To some extent, variations in terminology are the result of slightly different theoretical frameworks that have driven research within each area of problem behavior. As an illustration, consider the different language but common processes suggested by the theory of planned behavior that Charles and Blum discussed in Chapter Five and the social-cognitive information processing theories that Sullivan, Farrell, Bettencourt, and Helms discussed in Chapter Three: both address the centrality of normative beliefs about a behavior and self-efficacy to perform the behavior, but each has generated a somewhat separate strand of research.

The core competency framework was suggested as a mechanism to establish theoretical and empirical linkages across different research traditions within the risk-prevention and positive youth development literatures. Rather than select a specific theory or provide a laundry list of all risk factors, protective and promotive factors, or strengths, we tried to identify a limited number of broad competencies that were most central to the etiology and prevention of multiple problem behaviors and the promotion of adolescent well-being. As such, we highlighted five core competencies: a positive sense of self, self-control, decision-making skills, a moral system of belief, and prosocial connectedness. Our intent was to be inclusive enough to allow integration of different areas of emphasis within each type of risk behavior depending on the specific theories and processes that had guided previous research.

However, rather than delineating the core competencies and designing empirical studies to examine their relation to multiple outcomes prospectively, in some sense the authors were asked to work backward in order to fit prior research into this framework. Consequently, the competencies may have seemed a bit forced or perhaps a bit vague at some places in the volume. In addition, a lack of significant empirical findings may have been due to a lack of research in that area. For instance, few studies have examined the role of a moral system of belief in predicting early school leaving. But it may also be that some competencies are specific to some behaviors. For instance, a moral system of belief should be most relevant for violence and behaviors that harm others rather than behaviors that primarily harm the self.

Working forward requires that we examine the relative strength of each competency across multiple behaviors in order to identify the best approaches to prevention programming. For example, in a related study, Kim, Guerra, and Williams (2008) examined the role of a positive sense of self, self-control, decision making, and prosocial connectedness in predicting problem and health behaviors in a nationally representative sample of U.S. adolescents. Across these competencies, low self-control emerged as the strongest single predictor of problem behaviors and poor physical health outcomes.

With the exception of Chapter Six by Naudeau, Cunningham, Lundberg, and McGinnis, the chapter authors were asked to link the core competencies to a particular problem behavior. Although we proposed that the five core competencies reflect markers of social and emotional competence for adolescents that can reduce risk for multiple problem behaviors, we did not specify how they are linked to adjustment. This was complicated by a relative lack of specificity regarding psychological and behavioral markers of adjustment. In part, this is due to a lack of agreement on what it means to be successful in general or within a specific domain. For example, although the term *success at school* is commonly used by researchers, policymakers, and practitioners, a concise definition is lacking. Rather, most researchers operationalize school success as the absence of academic problems, truant behavior, or behavior problems at school.

Delineating more precise markers of healthy adjustment also has repercussions for specifying the acceptable boundaries for risk behaviors and directing preventive efforts. Several of the chapter authors acknowledged that some level of involvement in or experimentation with risk behavior is normative during adolescence (for instance, sexual activity, use of alcohol or other drugs, skipping school, and minor delinquency). This suggests that it is important to identify developmentally appropriate involvement in these risk domains and to differentiate prediction of normative experimentation from prediction of more serious levels of risk behaviors that are cause for concern and warrant a significant expenditure of prevention resources.

The central focus of this volume is on illustrating how the five individual-level competencies are linked specifically to four discrete problem behaviors and more generally to positive youth development. Our attention to individual competencies was not meant to minimize the significance of developmental and contextual influences on these emerging competencies. Many of the chapters specifically discuss how competencies unfold within specific contexts. For example, in Chapter Four, Haegerich and Tolan highlight the importance of families, peers, schools, culture, and society as socializing agents that can influence adolescents' core competencies and their substance use. Still, studies typically have focused on contextual predictors and outcomes or individual predictors and outcomes rather than on how contextual predictors influence individual predictors such as core competencies and, in turn, affect problem behavior and adjustment. A suggested next step is to examine more fully the context-competency-behavior link across time, setting, and culture.

We hope that this volume makes a small contribution to an ongoing dialogue that creates linkages within the field of youth problem behaviors and builds bridges between risk prevention and positive youth development approaches. Although we agree that problem free does not mean prepared, we propose that a common focus on core competencies can help youth become both problem free and prepared. Considering these as shared outcomes rather than casting them as rival approaches should ultimately result in integrated and coordinated policies and programs that benefit youth worldwide.

References

Kim, T. E., Guerra, N. G., & Williams, K. R. (2008). Preventing youth problem behaviors and enhancing physical health by promoting core competencies. *Journal of Adolescent Health, 43,* 401–407.

Pittman, K., Irby, M., Tolman, J., Yohalem, N., & Ferber, T. (2003). *Preventing problems, promoting development, encouraging engagement: Competing Priorities or inseparable goals?* Washington, DC: Forum for Youth Investment, Impact Strategies. Retrieved April 13, 2008, from www.forumfyi.org.

CATHERINE P. BRADSHAW *is an assistant professor and the associate director for the Johns Hopkins Center for the Prevention of Youth Violence at the Johns Hopkins Bloomberg School of Public Health.*

NANCY G. GUERRA *is a professor and the director of the Academic Center for Excellence in Youth Violence Prevention at the University of California, Riverside.*

INDEX

Abbey, A., 51
Abbott, R. D., 4, 24, 52
Aber, J. L., 40
Abide, M. M., 52
Agius, E., 51
Ainette, M. G., 51
Ajzen, I., 23, 63
Albarracin, D., 63
Albino, A., 36
Alessi, B., 82
Alvarado, R., 54
Amankwaa, L. I., 64
Anderson, C. A., 36
Arnett, J. J., 20
Aronowitz, T., 66
Arsenio, W. F., 36, 38
Arthur, M. W., 52
Atha, H., 40
August, G. J., 41
Austin, L., 10
Ayduk, O., 23

Bachman, J. G., 48
Bandura, A., 7, 8, 24, 51
Bang, H., 51
Barbaranelli, C., 24
Barber, B. K., 22
Barkin, S., 51
Battin-Pearson, S., 20, 21, 22, 24
Baumeister, R. F., 7, 9, 22, 36
Beam, M. R., 12
Behrman, R., 78
Bekman, S., 78
Bellamy, N., 52
Bender, D., 36
Benson, P. I., 3, 4, 11
Berglund, M. L., 4, 50
Berkel, C., 68
Berlinski, S., 79
Berman, S., 62
Bettencourt, A., 13, 33, 35, 46, 90
Bevans, K. B., 27
Beyers, J. M., 52
Beyth-Marom, R., 10
Bierman, K. L., 26
Biglan, A., 2
Bliesener, T., 36
Bloomquist, M. L., 41
Blum, R. W., 12, 13, 25, 61, 62, 74, 78, 79, 82

Boggess, S., 2
Bosch, J. D., 36
Botvin, G. J., 6, 51, 54
Bouchey, H., 22
Bowlby, J., 12, 24
Bowman, K., 80
Boxer, P., 40, 42, 55
Bradshaw, C. P., 1, 17, 19, 24, 27, 32, 89, 92
Braverman, P., 66
Breen, R., 54
Brennan, P. A., 2
Bresnick, S., 22
Brewster, K. L., 67
Brody, G. H., 50, 51, 68
Brofenbrenner, U., 5, 21, 63
Brookmeyer, K., 67
Brooks, L., 80
Brooks-Gunn, J., 67, 76
Brown, C. H., 40
Brown, J. L., 40
Brown, N. L., 64
Bryan, A., 50

Calvin, S., 48
Camou, S., 39, 40
Campbell, J. D., 7, 22
Campos, J. J., 36
Camras, L., 36
Capaldi, D., 55
Caprara, G. V., 24
Carlo, G., 38
Carlson, B., 21
Carter, J. A., 64
Carvajal, S. C., 51
Caspi, A., 9
Castellino, D. R., 35
Catalano, R. F., 4, 21, 24, 25, 35, 39, 50, 52
Cates, W., 62
Cauffman, E., 10
Cavanagh, S., 25
Charles, V., 13, 61, 74
Chassin, L., 48
Chatters, L. M., 53
Check & Connect mentoring program, 25–26
Chen, C., 12
Christenson, S., 25
Clinton, M., 51

93

Cnaan, R. A., 66
Coatsworth, J. D., 2, 5
Cohan, L., 76
Coie, J. D., 42
Commendador, K., 65
Competence, defined, 5
Conger, R. D., 67
Connectedness, 11–13, 24–25, 38–39, 52–53, 66–67
Connell, J. P., 23, 24
Connolly, J. A., 67
Connolly, J. A., 67
Conrad, J., 20
Constantine, J. M., 26
Cook, C. R., 55
Cooke, M. B., 40
Cooper, M. L., 36, 37
Coping Power program, 53–54
Core competencies: description of, 1, 8–13; future directions for research on, 89–92; school failure and, 19–28; sexual behavior and, 61–70; substance use and, 47–56; youth violence and, 33–43
Costa, F. M., 52
Cottrel, L., 66
Cowen, E. L., 4
Crane, J., 67
Crick, N. R., 10, 34, 36, 37, 38
Crocker, J., 8, 11
Crockett, L. J., 64
Crone, D. A., 26
Crosby, R. A., 66
Crosnoe, R., 25
Cross, S., 7
Crutchfield, C., 50
Culross, P., 78
Cunningham, W., 14, 75, 76, 77, 78, 79, 80, 81, 82, 83, 84, 87, 90, 91
Curnan, S., 3

Damon, W., 3
Davies, S., 66
Davis, L. E., 23
Day, L. E., 21, 35
De La Rosa, M., 55
Dean, R., 84
DeBaryshe, B. D., 21
Decision-making skills, 9–11, 23–24, 37, 51, 65
Dehne, K. L., 81
Demaray, M. K., 38
Diaz, T., 51, 54
DiClemente, R., 66
Diener, E., 8

Dishion, T. J., 55
Dodge, K. A., 10, 34, 36, 37, 38
Donahue, P. L., 27
Donaldson, S. I., 54
Drug and alcohol abuse. *See* Substance use
Dubow, E. F., 40, 42
Dunn, M., 53
DuRant, R. H., 48, 51

Eccles, J. S., 5, 12, 23, 51, 76
Eckstein, Z., 23
Edelstein, W., 12
Edwards, R. W., 52
Egeland, B., 21
Eisenberg, N., 38
Elder, G. H., 25, 67
Ellickson, P. L., 54
Embry, D. D., 40
Engels, R.C.M.E., 36
Ensminger, M. E., 21
Epstein, J. A., 51
Erikson, E., 7
Erwin, E. H., 35, 36, 42
Escobar, M., 65
Ethier, K. A., 64
Evans, A. E., 66
Evelo, D., 25

Fagan, J., 35
Falci, C., 24
Farley, F., 10
Farrell, A. D., 13, 33, 35, 36, 39, 40, 42, 46, 90
Farrington, D. P., 2
Fearnow-Kenney, M., 51
Feldman, S. S., 64
Ferber, T., 90
Fernald, L., 84
Filter, K. J., 26
Finkenauer, C., 36
Finn, J. D., 22, 23
Fischhoff, B., 10
Fishbein, D. H., 51
Fishbein, M., 63
Flanagan, C., 81
Flannery, D. J., 40
Flay, B. R., 49
Fleming, C. B., 24, 39
Fong, G. T., 66
Fontaine, R. G., 36, 37, 38
Forehand, R., 63, 64
Fortier, M. S., 22
Foster, S. L., 2
Foxcroft, D. R., 54

Foy, P., 79
Frank, D., 64
Frankel, C. B., 36
Franklin, C., 28
French, D. C., 20
Frey, K. S., 40
Frick, P. J., 38
Furstenburg, F. F., Jr., 65

Galbraith, J., 66
Galiani, S., 79
Garbarino, J., 24
Garcia-Nunez, J., 81
Garcia-Verdu, R., 76
Gardner, I. H., 64
Garnier, H. E., 20, 24
Gauthier, Y., 38
Ge, X., 51
Gelles, R. J., 66
Geronimus, A. T., 65
Gerrard, M., 51, 68
Gertler, P., 79
Gestsdottir, S., 9
Gibbons, F. X., 51, 68
Gibson, E., 6
Giedd, J. N., 9
Gilmore, M. R., 21
Glantz, M. D., 49
Goldstein, A. P., 6
Goldstein, S. E., 42
Gomby, D., 78
Gomez, R., 38
Gonzalez-Soldevilla, A., 66
Gootman, J., 5, 12, 76
Gorman-Smith, D., 39, 49, 53
Gottfredson, M. R., 9, 37, 54
Graham, J. W., 54
Graham, S., 34
Grantham-McGregor, S., 79, 83
Greenberg, M. T., 26
Greenberger, E., 12
Griffin, K. W., 51, 54
Grigg, W. S., 27
Grillo, G. P., 62
Grossman, D. C., 26
Grotpeter, J. K., 6, 25
Guay, F., 22
Guerra, N. G., 1, 5, 10, 11, 17, 34, 35, 36, 38, 42, 49, 55, 80, 89, 91, 92
Guo, J., 52
Guzzo, B. A., 40

Haegerich, T. M., 13, 47, 60, 92
Haggerty, K. P., 24, 39, 54
Hahn, A., 80
Hahn, R., 39, 40
Hair, E., 25
Hammond, W. R., 41
Hanish, L. D., 35
Hansen, W. B., 50, 51, 54
Harlan, E. A., 62
Harlan, W. R., 62
Harmoni, R., 65
Harrington, K. F., 66
Harrison, K., 51
Hart, B., 66
Harter, S., 6, 7, 22, 67
Harter, S., 67
Havighurst, R. J., 5
Hawken, L. S., 26
Hawkins, D., 52
Hawkins, J. D., 4, 21, 24, 35, 39, 50, 52, 54
Hektner, J. M., 41
Helms, S. W., 33, 46, 90
Henrich, C. C., 67
Henry, D. B., 39
Henry, G., 9
Henry, K. L., 50, 52, 53
Hepler, N., 50
Heretick, D., 42
Higgins-D'Alessandro, A., 52
Hill, K. G., 4, 24, 52
Hilton, I., 66
Hingson, R., 48
Hirschi, T., 9
Hirschstein, M. K., 40
Hobbie, W. L., 65
Hofman, V., 12
Holder, H. D., 2
Hollen, P. J., 65
Horner, R. H., 26, 27
Huesmann, L. R., 10, 11, 38
Hughes, D., 3
Hurley, C., 25
Hüsler, G., 52
Hutchinson, M. K., 66, 67

Ialongo, N., 27, 40
Iffil-Williams, M., 54
Individuals with Disabilities in Education Act, 27
International perspective on positive youth development, 75–85
Irby, M., 3, 90
Ireland, D., 54

Jacobs, J. K., 20
Jacobsen, T., 12
Jacobs-Quadrel, M., 10

James, S., 52
Jang, S. J., 53
Jekielek, S., 25
Jemmott, J. B., 63, 64, 66
Jemmott, L. S., 63, 64
Jensen, R., 82
Jessor, R., 2, 3, 49, 52, 69
Jessor, S. L., 3, 49
Jimerson, S. R., 21
Johnson, B. R., 53
Johnson, B. T., 63
Johnson, L., 82
Johnston, L., 48, 49
Jones, M., 80
Jones, S. M., 40
Juvonen, J., 34

Kagitcibasi, C., 78
Kaljee, L., 66
Kao, M., 67
Kegeles, S. M., 64
Kellam, S. G., 40
Kelly, F. D., 20, 25, 28
Kemple, J. J., 27
Kendall, P. C., 49
Kenkel, D., 48
Kennedy, A., 79
Kim, J. S., 28
Kim, S., 50
Kim, T. E., 91
King, K. M., 48
Kirby, D., 12, 63, 68, 69
Kitayama, S., 5
Klem, A. M., 24
Knauth, D. G., 65
Kogan, S. M., 50, 52
Kohlberg, L., 38
Komro, K. A., 54
Konarski, R., 67
Koops, W., 36
Kopp, C. B., 8
Kosterman, R., 4, 24, 52, 54
Kotchick, B. A., 63, 64
Koth, C. W., 27
Kowaleski-Jones, L., 64
Kramer, R., 38
Kreiter, S. R., 48
Krop, R. A., 20
Krowchuk, D. P., 48
Krueger, J. I., 7, 22
Ku, L., 67
Kuendig, H., 52
Kumpfer, K. L., 54
Kung, E., 40

Kuntsche, E. N., 52
Kusché, C., 26
Kuther, T. L., 52
Kuttler, A. F., 67
Kuttler, A. F., 67

La Greca, A. M., 67
Laible, D. J., 38
Lanspery, S., 80
Larson, R. W., 3
Leaf, P. J., 27
Leavitt, T., 80
Leffert, N., 3
Leidy, M., 5
Lemerise, E. A., 36, 38
Lemmon, K., 7
Lerner, R. M., 3, 4, 9, 35, 76, 81, 84
Leshner, A. I., 49
Levene, K. S., 34
Levenstein, P., 26
Levenstein, S., 26
Li, F., 55
Li, X., 66
Life skills, 80
Lindberg, L. D., 2
Ling, X., 40
Lipsey, M. W., 39, 40, 41
Lister-Sharp, D. J., 54
Lochman, J. E., 38, 53, 54
Lochman, L. E., 54
Lochner, L., 20
Loeber, R., 2
Lonczak, H. S., 4, 50
Longshore, D., 54
Losel, F., 36
Loveder, P., 80
Lowe, G., 54
Ludden, A. B., 51
Ludwig, K. B., 35
Luker, K., 65
Lundberg, M.K.A., 14, 75, 87, 90, 91
Luo, Z., 50

Madsen, K. C., 34
Malecki, C. K., 38
Mallonee, E., 48
Mangrulkar, L., 80
Mann, L., 65
Marcus, R. F., 24
Markus, H., 5, 7
Martin, A., 81
Martin, E. S., 26
Martin, M., 79
Mason, W. A., 54

Masten, A. S., 2, 5, 67
Matthew, R. F., 52
Mays, S., 36, 42
McBride, A. M., 82
McCaffrey, D. F., 54
McCree, D. H., 66
McGee, R. O., 9
McGill, D. E., 25
McGinnis, L., 14, 75, 76, 87, 90, 91
McLaren, S., 38
McMahon, S. D., 40
McNair, L. D., 64
McNeal, R. B., 50, 51
McNeely, C. A., 12, 13, 19, 22, 24, 25, 32
Meehan, B. T., 48
Meekers, D., 83
Memmo, M., 3
Mendoza, D., 51
Merisca, R., 40
Merk, W., 36
Merten, M. J., 67
Meyer, A. L., 40
Midgely, C., 12
Mihalic, S. F., 6, 25, 26
Miller, J. T., 81
Miller, J. Y., 50
Miller, K. S., 63, 64
Miller, T. Q., 49
Mirabel-Colon, B., 5
Mischel, W., 22, 23
Moffitt, T. E., 9, 34
Moore, C., 7
Moore, K. A., 25
Moral system of belief, 11, 24, 38, 52, 65–66
Moretti, E., 20
Morris, K., 48
Morris, P., 5, 21
Morrison, D. M., 35
Mott, F. L., 64
Muellerleile, P. A., 63
Mullis, I., 79
Muraven, M., 9
Murray, M., 54
Murry, V. M., 50, 67, 68, 69
Musher-Eizenman, D., 42
Myers, D., 26

Namerow, P. B., 65
Naudeau, S., 14, 75, 76, 87, 90, 91
Nelson, D. A., 37
Newcomb, M. D., 20, 52
Newcomer, S. F., 66
Nisan, M., 11

No Child Left Behind (NCLB) act, 27
Nonnemaker, J. M., 12, 25
Northup, W., 40
Nucci, L., 11, 38

O'Brennan, L., 13, 19, 32
O'Donnell, J., 35
O'Donnell, L., 68
Oesterle, S., 24, 39
Okonofua, F. E., 81
Olate, R., 82
O'Malley, P. M., 48
Oman, R. F., 50, 52, 53
O'Neal, K. K., 53
Orcutt, H. K., 36
Orlando, M., 54
Orobio de Castro, B., 36
O'Sullivan, L. F., 67
Overby, K. J., 64

Palardy, G, 27, 28
Palmgren, C., 10
Pantin, H., 66
Pardini, D. A., 38
Pastorelli, C., 24
Patterson, G. R., 21
Pepler, D. J., 34
Perie, M., 27
Perrino, T., 66
Perry, J., 82
Petraitis, J., 49
Petrow, J., 79
Phillips, D., 79
Philiber, S., 65
Pianta, R. C., 27
Pittman, J. F., 35
Pittman, K., 3, 90
Plancherel, B., 52
Plautz, A., 83
Pleck, J. H., 67
Plybon, L., 40
Pollard, J. A., 50
Positive Behavioral Interventions and Supports (PBIS), 27
Positive sense of self, 6–8, 22, 35–36, 50–51, 63–64
Positive youth development, 3
Posner, M., 80
Powell, K. E., 40
Power, C., 65
Prevatt, F., 20, 25, 28
Prinstein, M. J., 67
Prosocial connectedness, 11–13, 24–25, 38–39, 52–53, 66–67

Rabiner, D. L., 38
Raffaelli, M., 38, 64
Raikes, A., 84
Ramsay, S. G., 52
Ramsey, E., 21
Realmuto, G. M., 41
Reitman, D., 64
Rennells, R. E., 66
Reproductive health services, youth-friendly, 81
Resnick, M. D., 66, 67
Reyna, V. F., 10
Richards, H. C., 52
Riedner, G., 81
Rinehart, P., 78
Ripple, C. H., 2
Risk behaviors, 2
Robbins, R. N., 50
Rock, D. A., 22, 23
Rodgers, J. L., 67
Rodgers, J. L., 67
Rodriguez, M., 22
Rohde, P., 48, 50
Ronis, D. L., 63
Roth, J. L., 76
Rowe, D. C., 67
Rumberger, R. W., 27, 28
Rutter, M., 21
Ryan, J.A.M., 4, 50
Rydell, C. P., 20

Salazar, L. F., 64
Sambrano, S., 53
Sanders-Reio, J., 24
Saunders, J., 23, 80
Scales, P. C., 3
Scheier, L. M., 51
Schenkl, P., 81
School failure and early school leaving, 19–28
Schulenberg, J. E., 48
Schwartz, D., 36
Schweinhart, L. J., 26, 79
Seftor, N. S., 26
Self-awareness, 6
Self-control, 8–9, 22–23, 36–37, 51, 64
Senderowitz, J., 81
Sexual behavior, high-risk, 61–70
Shaffer, A., 63
Shahar, G., 67
Shears, J., 52
Shen, Y. L., 64
Shepard, B. L., 81
Sherraden, M., 82

Sherrod, L., 81
Shiminski, J. A., 26
Shoda, Y., 22
Shonkoff, J., 79
Shrier, L. A., 67
Silva, P. A., 9
Silva, T., 26
Simmons, P. S., 62
Simons, R. L., 67
Sinclair, M., 25
Sinha, J. W., 66
Skara, S., 54
Skinner, E. A., 23
Skowron, E. A., 65
Slater, M. D., 50
Slusarcick, A. L., 21
Small, S., 3
Smith, E. P., 5, 36
Smith, J. A., 48
Smith, K. S., 51
Snipes, J. C., 27
Sobeck, J., 51
Sonenstein, F. L., 67
Spoth, R. L., 54
Spracklen, K. M., 55
Sroufe, L. A., 21
Stanback, J., 81
Stanley, L. R., 52
Stanton, B., 66
Stein, J. A., 20
Steinberg, L., 9, 10, 48
Stokes, H., 80
Stolzberg, J. E., 26
Stouthamer-Loeber, M., 2
Streeter, C. L., 28
Substance use, prevention of, 47–56
Sullivan, T., 13, 33, 46, 90
Sunar, D., 78
Sussman, S., 54
Swaim, R. C., 50
Szapocznik, J., 66

Tait, C., 54
Tarter, R. E., 53
Teliuc, C., 76
Thompson, R. A., 8, 9
Thurlow, M., 25
Tidwell, R. P., 40
Tobler, N. S., 54
Todd, E., 66
Tolan, P. H., 13, 34, 39, 42, 47, 48, 49, 53, 54, 55, 60, 92
Tolman, J., 90
Tosh, A. K., 62

Toumbourou, J. W., 52
Transgrud, R., 81
Trenholm, C., 69
Trim, R. S., 48
Tripodi, S. J., 28
Turbin, M. S., 52
Turiel, E., 38
Twum-Baah, K. A., 81
Tyler, D., 80

Udry, J. R., 66

Vallerand, R. J., 22
Valois, R. F., 40
van Ijzendoorn, M. H., 38
Vazsonyi, A. T., 40
Veerman, J. W., 36
Vegas, E., 79
Velez, C., 5
Verner, D., 76
Vernez, G., 2
Vernon, R., 81
Villarruel, A. M., 63, 64
Violence, youth, 33–43
Vohs, K. D., 7, 22
Vulin-Reynolds, M., 42

Walberg, H. J., 24
Walker, C., 51
Wang, M. C., 24
Wang, M. Q., 52
Washburn, J. J., 40
Watson, J., 7
Webster, C., 34
Wei, E., 2
Weinstock, H., 62
Weis, J. G., 4
Weissberg, R. P., 24
Wellborn, J. G., 23

Wells, K. C., 53, 54
Wentzel, K. R., 24
Werlen, E., 52
West, S. L., 53
Whitbeck, L. B., 67
Whitbeck, L. B., 67
Whitesell, N. R., 22
Whiteside, H. O., 54
Whitlock, J., 12
Whitman, C., 80
Wickrama, K.A.S., 67
Wigfield, A., 24
Wikström, P. H., 2
Wilkinson, D. L., 35
Williams, C., 50
Williams, K. R., 91
Williams, M. K., 64
Williams, S., 2
Williams, T., 23
Wills, T. A., 51, 52
Wilson, D. B., 54
Wilson, S. J., 39, 40, 41
Wingood, G. M., 66
Wolfe, C. T., 8, 11
Wolfe, K., 81
Wolpin, K. I., 23
Wood, E. B., 66
Wood, P. K., 36
Wyn, J., 80

Yang, H., 66
Youniss, J., 81
Youth violence, prevention of, 33–43
Yung, B. R., 41

Zhou, X. K., 51
Zigler, E., 2
Zimbardo, P. G., 24
Zimmer-Gembeck, M. J., 23
Zins, J. E., 24

OTHER TITLES AVAILABLE IN THE
NEW DIRECTIONS FOR CHILD AND ADOLESCENT DEVELOPMENT SERIES
Reed W. Larson and Lene Arnett Jensen, Editors-in-Chief
William Damon, Founding Editor-in-Chief

For a complete list of back issues, please visit www.josseybass..com/go/ndcad

CAD 121 **Beyond the Family: Contexts of Immigrant Children's Development**
Hirokazu Yoshikawa, Niobe Way, Editors
Immigration in the United States has become a central focus of policy and public concern in the first decade of the 21st century. This volume aims to broaden developmental research on children and youth in immigrant families. Much of the research on immigrant children and youth concentrates on family characteristics such as parenting, demographic, or human capital features. In this volume, we consider the developmental consequences for immigrant youth of broader contexts such as social networks, peer discrimination in school and out-of-school settings, legal contexts, and access to institutional resources. Chapters answer questions such as: How do experiences of discrimination affect the lives of immigrant youth? How do social networks of immigrant families influence children's learning? How do immigrant parents' citizenship status influence family life and their children's development? In examining factors as disparate as discrimination based on physical appearance, informal adult helpers, and access to drivers' licenses, these chapters serve to enrich our notions of how culture and context shape human development, as well as inform practice and public policy affecting immigrant families.
ISBN 978-04704-17300

CAD 120 **The Intersections of Personal and Social Identities**
Margarita Azmitia, Moin Syed, Kimberley Radmacher, Editors
This volume brings together an interdisciplinary set of social scientists who are pioneering ways to research and theorize the connections between personal and social identity development in children, adolescents, and emerging adults. The authors of the seven chapters address the volume's three goals: (1) illustrating how theory and research in identity develop-ment are enriched by an interdisciplinary approach, (2) providing a rich developmental picture of personal and social identity development, and (3) examining the connections among multiple identities. Several chapters provide practical suggestions for individuals, agencies, and schools and universities that work with children, adolescents, and emerging adults in diverse communities across the United States.
ISBN 978-04703-72838

CAD 119 **Social Class and Transitions to Adulthood**
Jeylan T. Mortimer, Editor
This volume of *New Directions for Child and Adolescent Development* is inspired by a stirring address that Frank Furstenberg delivered at the 2006 Meeting of the Society for Research on Adolescence, "Diverging Development: The Not So Invisible Hand of Social Class in the United States." He called on social

scientists interested in the study of development to expand their purview beyond investigations of the developmental impacts of poverty and consider the full gamut of social class variation in our increasingly unequal society. The gradations of class alter the social supports, resources, and opportunities, as well as the constraints, facing parents as they attempt to guide their children toward the acquisition of adult roles. This volume examines the impacts of social class origin on the highly formative period of transition to adulthood. Drawing on findings from the Youth Development Study and other sources, the authors examine social class differences in adult child–parent relationships, intimacy and family formation, attainment of higher education, the school-to-work transition, the emergence of work-family conflict, and harassment in the workplace. The authors indicate new directions for research that will contribute to understanding the problems facing young people today. These chapters will persuade those making social policy to develop social interventions that will level the playing field and increase the opportunities for disadvantaged youth to become healthy and productive adults.
ISBN 978-04702-93621

CAD 118 **Social Network Analysis and Children's Peer Relationships**
Philip C. Rodkin, Laura D. Hanish, Editors
Social network analysis makes it possible to determine how large and dense children's peer networks are, how central children are within their networks, the various structural configurations that characterize social groups, and which peers make up individual children's networks. By centering the child within his or her social system, it is possible to understand the socialization processes that draw children toward or away from particular peers, as well as those who contribute to peer influence. This volume of *New Directions for Child and Adolescent Development* demonstrates how social network analysis provides insights into the ways in which peer groups contribute to children's and adolescents' development—from gender and intergroup relations, to aggression and bullying, to academic achievement. Together the chapters in this volume depict the complex, nested, and dynamic structure of peer groups and explain how social structure defines developmental processes.
ISBN 978-04702-59665

CAD 117 **Attachment in Adolescence: Reflections and New Angles**
Miri Scharf, Ofra Mayseless, Editors
In recent years, the number of empirical studies examining attachment in adolescence has grown considerably, with most focusing on individual differences in attachment security. This volume goes a step further in extending our knowledge and understanding. The physical, cognitive, emotional, and social changes that characterize adolescence invite a closer conceptual look at attachment processes and organization during this period. The chapter authors, leading researchers in attachment in adolescence, address key topics in attachment processes in adolescence. These include issues such as the normative distancing from parents and the growing importance of peers, the formation of varied attachment hierarchies, the changing nature of attachment dynamics from issues of survival to issues of affect regulation, siblings' similarity in attachment representations, individual differences in social information processes in adolescence, and stability and change in attachment representations in a risk sample. Together the chapters provide a compelling discussion of intriguing issues and broaden our understanding of attachment in adolescence and the basic tenets of attachment theory at large.
ISBN 978-04702-25608

CAD 116 **Linking Parents and Family to Adolescent Peer Relations: Ethnic and Cultural Considerations**
B. Bradford Brown, Nina S. Mounts, Editors
Ethnic and cultural background shapes young people's development and behavior in a variety of ways, including their interactions with family and peers. The intersection of family and peer worlds during childhood has been studied extensively, but only recently has this work been extended to adolescence. This volume of *New Directions for Child and Adolescent Development* highlights new research linking family to adolescent peer relations from a multiethnic perspective. Using qualitative and quantitative research methods, the contributors consider similarities and differences within and between ethnic groups in regard to several issues: parents' goals and strategies for guiding young people to adaptive peer relationships, how peer relationships shape and are shaped by kin relationships, and the specific strategies that adolescents and parents use to manage information about peers or negotiate rules about peer interactions and relationships. Findings emphasize the central role played by sociocultural context in shaping the complex, bidirectional processes that link family members to adolescents' peer social experiences.
ISBN 978-04701-78010

CAD 115 **Conventionality in Cognitive Development: How Children Acquire Shared Representations in Language, Thought, and Action**
Chuck W. Kalish, Mark A. Sabbagh, Editors
An important part of cognitive development is coming to think in culturally normative ways. Children learn the right names for objects, proper functions for tools, appropriate ways to categorize, and the rules for games. In each of these cases, what makes a given practice normative is not naturally given. There is not necessarily any objectively better or worse way to do any of these things. Instead, what makes them correct is that people agree on how they should be done, and each of these practices therefore has an important conventional basis. The chapters in this volume highlight the fact that successful participation in practices of language, cognition, and play depends on children's ability to acquire representations that other members of their social worlds share. Each of these domains poses problems of identifying normative standards and achieving coordination across agents. This volume brings together scholars from diverse areas in cognitive development to consider the psychological mechanisms supporting the use and acquisition of conventional knowledge.
ISBN 978-07879-96970

CAD 114 **Respect and Disrespect: Cultural and Developmental Origins**
David W. Schwalb, Barbara J. Schwalb, Editors
Respect enables children and teenagers to value other people, institutions, traditions, and themselves. Disrespect is the agent that dissolves positive relationships and fosters hostile and cynical relationships. Unfortunately, parents, educators, children, and adolescents in many societies note with alarm a growing problem of disrespect and a decline in respect for self and others. Is this disturbing trend a worldwide problem? To answer this question, we must begin to study the developmental and cultural origins of respect and disrespect. Five research teams report that respect and disrespect are influenced by experiences in the family, school, community, and, most importantly, the broader cultural setting. The chapters introduce a new topic area for mainstream developmental sciences that is relevant to the interests of scholars, educators, practitioners, and policymakers.
ISBN 978-07879-95584

CAD 113 **The Modernization of Youth Transitions in Europe**
Manuela du Bois-Reymond, Lynne Chisholm, Editors
This compelling volume focuses on what it is like to be young in the rapidly changing, enormously diverse world region that is early 21st century Europe. Designed for a North American readership interested in youth and young adulthood, *The Modernization of Youth Transitions in Europe* provides a rich fund of theoretical insight and empirical evidence about the implications of contemporary modernization processes for young people living, learning, and working across Europe. Chapters have been specially written for this volume by well-known youth sociologists; they cover a wide range of themes against a shared background of the reshaping of the life course and its constituent phases toward greater openness and contigency. New modes of learning accompany complex routes into employment and career under rapidly changing labor market conditions and occupational profiles, while at the same time new family and lifestyle forms are developing alongside greater intergenerational responsibilities in the face of the retreat of the modern welfare state. The complex patterns of change for today's young Europeans are set into a broader framework that analyzes the emergence and character of European youth research and youth policy in recent years.
ISBN 978-07879-88890

CAD 112 **Rethinking Positive Adolescent Female Sexual Development**
Lisa M. Diamond, Editor
This volume provides thoughtful and diverse perspectives on female adolescent sexuality. These perspectives integrate biological, cultural, and interpersonal influences on adolescent girls' sexuality, and highlight the importance of using multiple methods to investigate sexual ideation and experience. Traditional portrayals cast adolescent females as sexual gatekeepers whose primary task is to fend off boys' sexual overtures and set aside their own sexual desires in order to reduce their risks for pregnancy and sexually transmitted diseases. Yet an increasing number of thoughtful and constructive critiques have challenged this perspective, arguing for more sensitive, in-depth, multimethod investigations into the positive meanings of sexuality for adolescent girls that will allow us to conceptualize (and, ideally, advocate for) healthy sexual-developmental trajectories. Collectively, authors of this volume take up this movement and chart exciting new directions for the next generation of developmental research on adolescent female sexuality.
ISBN 978-07879-87350

NEW DIRECTIONS FOR CHILD & ADOLESCENT DEVELOPMENT
ORDER FORM — SUBSCRIPTION AND SINGLE ISSUES

DISCOUNTED BACK ISSUES:

Use this form to receive 20% off all back issues of *New Directions for Child & Adolescent Development*. All single issues priced at **$23.20** (normally $29.00)

TITLE　　　　　　　　　　　　　　　ISSUE NO.　　　　ISBN

_____　_____　_____
_____　_____　_____
_____　_____　_____

Call 888-378-2537 or see mailing instructions below. When calling, mention the promotional code JB9ND to receive your discount. For a complete list of issues, please visit www.josseybass.com/go/ndcad

SUBSCRIPTIONS: (1 YEAR, 4 ISSUES)

☐ New Order　　☐ Renewal

U.S.	☐ Individual: $85	☐ Institutional: $280
Canada/Mexico	☐ Individual: $85	☐ Institutional: $320
All Others	☐ Individual: $109	☐ Institutional: $354

Call 888-378-2537 or see mailing and pricing instructions below.
Online subscriptions are available at www.interscience.wiley.com

ORDER TOTALS:

Issue / Subscription Amount: $ _____

Shipping Amount: $ _____
(for single issues only – subscription prices include shipping)

Total Amount: $ _____

SHIPPING CHARGES:

SURFACE	DOMESTIC	CANADIAN
First Item	$5.00	$6.00
Each Add'l Item	$3.00	$1.50

(No sales tax for U.S. subscriptions. Canadian residents, add GST for subscription orders. Individual rate subscriptions must be paid by personal check or credit card. Individual rate subscriptions may not be resold as library copies.)

BILLING & SHIPPING INFORMATION:

☐ **PAYMENT ENCLOSED:** *(U.S. check or money order only. All payments must be in U.S. dollars.)*

☐ **CREDIT CARD:**　☐ VISA　☐ MC　☐ AMEX

Card number _____ Exp. Date _____

Card Holder Name _____ Card Issue # _____

Signature _____ Day Phone _____

☐ **BILL ME:** *(U.S. institutional orders only. Purchase order required.)*

Purchase order # _____
　　　　　　　Federal Tax ID 13559302 • GST 89102-8052

Name _____
Address _____
Phone _____ E-mail _____

Copy or detach page and send to:　**John Wiley & Sons, PTSC, 5th Floor**
　　　　　　　　　　　　　　　　　989 Market Street, San Francisco, CA 94103-1741

Order Form can also be faxed to:　**888-481-2665**

PROMO JB9ND

NEW DIRECTIONS FOR CHILD AND ADOLESCENT DEVELOPMENT IS NOW AVAILABLE ONLINE AT WILEY INTERSCIENCE

What is Wiley InterScience?

Wiley InterScience is the dynamic online content service from John Wiley & Sons delivering the full text of over 300 leading scientific, technical, medical, and professional journals, plus major reference works, the acclaimed Current Protocols laboratory manuals, and even the full text of select Wiley print books online.

What are some special features of Wiley InterScience?

Wiley Interscience Alerts is a service that delivers table of contents via e-mail for any journal available on Wiley InterScience as soon as a new issue is published online.
EarlyView is Wiley's exclusive service presenting individual articles online as soon as they are ready, even before the release of the compiled print issue. These articles are complete, peer-reviewed, and citable.
CrossRef is the innovative multi-publisher reference linking system enabling readers to move seamlessly from a reference in a journal article to the cited publication, typically located on a different server and published by a different publisher.

How can I access Wiley InterScience?

Visit http://www.interscience.wiley.com.

Guest Users can browse Wiley InterScience for unrestricted access to journal tables of contents and article abstracts, or use the powerful search engine.
Registered Users are provided with a *Personal Home Page* to store and manage customized alerts, searches, and links to favorite journals and articles. Additionally, Registered Users can view free online sample issues and preview selected material from major reference works.
Licensed Customers are entitled to access full-text journal articles in PDF, with select journals also offering full-text HTML.

How do I become an Authorized User?

Authorized Users are individuals authorized by a paying Customer to have access to the journals in Wiley InterScience. For example, a university that subscribes to Wiley journals is considered to be the Customer.
Faculty, staff, and students authorized by the university to have access to those journals in Wiley InterScience are Authorized Users. Users should contact their library for information on which Wiley journals they have access to in Wiley InterScience.

ASK YOUR INSTITUTION ABOUT WILEY INTERSCIENCE TODAY!

Statement of Ownership, Management, and Circulation
(All Periodicals Publications Except Requester Publications)

UNITED STATES POSTAL SERVICE

1. Publication Title	2. Publication Number	3. Filing Date
New Directions for Child and Adolescent Development	1520-3247	10/1/2008

4. Issue Frequency	5. Number of Issues Published Annually	6. Annual Subscription Price
Quarterly	4	$258

7. Complete Mailing Address of Known Office of Publication (Not printer) (Street, city, county, state, and ZIP+4®)	Contact Person
Wiley Subscriptions Services, Inc. at Jossey-Bass, 989 Market St., San Francisco, CA 94103	Joe Schuman
	Telephone (Include area code) 415-782-3232

8. Complete Mailing Address of Headquarters or General Business Office of Publisher (Not printer)

Wiley Subscriptions Services, Inc., 111 River Street, Hoboken, NJ 07030

9. Full Names and Complete Mailing Addresses of Publisher, Editor, and Managing Editor (Do not leave blank)

Publisher (Name and complete mailing address)

Wiley Subscriptions Services, Inc., A Wiley Company at San Francisco, 989 Market St., San Francisco, CA 94103-1741

Editor (Name and complete mailing address)

Co-Editor - Reed Larson, Dept. of Human & Community Devel., Univ. of Illinois, 1105 W. Nevada St., Urbana IL 61801

Managing Editor (Name and complete mailing address)

Co-Editor - Dr. Lene Arnett Jensen, Ph.D., Clark University, Dept. of Psychology, 950 Main St., Worcester, MA 01610

10. Owner (Do not leave blank. If the publication is owned by a corporation, give the name and address of the corporation immediately followed by the names and addresses of all stockholders owning or holding 1 percent or more of the total amount of stock. If not owned by a corporation, give the names and addresses of the individual owners. If owned by a partnership or other unincorporated firm, give its name and address as well as those of each individual owner. If the publication is published by a nonprofit organization, give its name and address.)

Full Name	Complete Mailing Address
Wiley Subscriptions Services	111 River Street, Hoboken, NJ
(see attached list)	

11. Known Bondholders, Mortgagees, and Other Security Holders Owning or Holding 1 Percent or More of Total Amount of Bonds, Mortgages, or Other Securities. If none, check box ► ☑ None

Full Name	Complete Mailing Address

12. Tax Status (For completion by nonprofit organizations authorized to mail at nonprofit rates) (Check one)
The purpose, function, and nonprofit status of this organization and the exempt status for federal income tax purposes:
☐ Has Not Changed During Preceding 12 Months
☐ Has Changed During Preceding 12 Months (Publisher must submit explanation of change with this statement)

13. Publication Title	14. Issue Date for Circulation Data
New Directions for Child and Adolescent Development	Summer 2008

15. Extent and Nature of Circulation			Average No. Copies Each Issue During Preceding 12 Months	No. Copies of Single Issue Published Nearest to Filing Date
a. Total Number of Copies (Net press run)			753	729
b. Paid Circulation (By Mail and Outside the Mail)	(1)	Mailed Outside-County Paid Subscriptions Stated on PS Form 3541 (Include paid distribution above nominal rate, advertiser's proof copies, and exchange copies)	187	189
	(2)	Mailed In-County Paid Subscriptions Stated on PS Form 3541 (Include paid distribution above nominal rate, advertiser's proof copies, and exchange copies)	0	0
	(3)	Paid Distribution Outside the Mails Including Sales Through Dealers and Carriers, Street Vendors, Counter Sales, and Other Paid Distribution Outside USPS®	0	0
	(4)	Paid Distribution by Other Classes of Mail Through the USPS (e.g. First-Class Mail®)	0	0
c. Total Paid Distribution (Sum of 15b (1), (2), (3), and (4))			187	189
d. Free or Nominal Rate Distribution (By Mail and Outside the Mail)	(1)	Free or Nominal Rate Outside-County Copies included on PS Form 3541	43	44
	(2)	Free or Nominal Rate In-County Copies Included on PS Form 3541	0	0
	(3)	Free or Nominal Rate Copies Mailed at Other Classes Through the USPS (e.g. First-Class Mail)	0	0
	(4)	Free or Nominal Rate Distribution Outside the Mail (Carriers or other means)	0	0
e. Total Free or Nominal Rate Distribution (Sum of 15d (1), (2), (3) and (4))			43	44
f. Total Distribution (Sum of 15c and 15e)		►	230	233
g. Copies not Distributed (See Instructions to Publishers #4 (page #3))		►	523	496
h. Total (Sum of 15f and g)		►	753	729
i. Percent Paid (15c divided by 15f times 100)		►	81%	81%

16. Publication of Statement of Ownership.
☐ If the publication is a general publication, publication of this statement is required. Will be printed in the Winter 2008 issue of this publication.
☐ Publication not required.

17. Signature and Title of Editor, Publisher, Business Manager, or Owner	Date
Susan E. Lewis, VP & Publisher - Periodicals	10/1/2008

I certify that all information furnished on this form is true and complete. I understand that anyone who furnishes false or misleading information on this form or who omits material or information requested on the form may be subject to criminal sanctions (including fines and imprisonment) and/or civil sanctions (including civil penalties).